W9-DFW-581

THE FATHER Book
Pregnancy and Beyond

THE FATHER Book
Pregnancy and Beyond

by Rae Grad, R.N., Ph.D.
Deborah Bash, C.N.M.
Ruth Guyer, Ph.D.
Zoila Acevedo, R.N., Ph.D.
Mary Anne Trause, Ph.D.
Diane Reukauf, M.A.

The Alliance for Perinatal Research and Services, Inc.

Foreword by Frank Pedersen, Ph.D.
National Institute of Child Health
and Human Development

Photographs by Cindy Johnson

ACROPOLIS BOOKS LTD.
2400 17th Street, N.W. Washington, D.C. 20009

Dedication

To our husbands and children—John, Arlen, Rebecca, Aaron, Marvin, Robert, Gila, Alan, Jeremy, Mark, Anya, Dana, Jose, Eric, Paul, Amanda, Bill, Beth Anne, Kathryn, and Michael—we love you.

ACROPOLIS BOOKS LTD.
Colortone Building, 2400 17th St., N.W.
Washington, D.C. 20009

Printed in the United States of America by
COLORTONE PRESS, Creative Graphics Inc.
Washington, D.C. 20009

Library of Congress Cataloging in Publication Data
Main entry under title:

The father book.

Bibliography: p.
Includes index.
1. Pregnancy. 2. Childbirth. 3. Fathers.
I. Alliance for Perinatal Research and Services
(U.S.) II. Title.
RG525.F37 649'.1 80-27800
ISBN 0-87491-618-6
ISBN 0-87491-422-1 (pbk.)

Contents

Foreword

For many years, both social scientists and fathers themselves viewed the father's position in the family as primarily the provider of economic resources. If, in addition, a father played with the children, exercised discipline, and was kind and loving toward his wife, that was a bonus. I believe the single most powerful influence that enlarged this narrow conception of family roles was the natural childbirth movement. Perhaps more appropriately labeled participative or prepared childbirth, educational and childbirth preparation groups have focused efforts on reducing medical intervention during childbirth and encouraging a close, nurturing relationship between parents and child. The key element in bringing about this change has been the restoration of significant social relationships in the childbirth setting. Labor and delivery now most often occur in the presence of a trained and emotionally supportive person, most frequently the father who attended childbirth preparation classes. Rooming-in arrangements in the post-delivery period are vastly more prevalent, and efforts have been made to minimize the separations between mother, father and infant that often occurred in the hospital setting. Initially these changes were made in the interest of promoting more optimal circumstances for the infant, as well as a more favorable relationship between mother and infant.

A parallel and possibly more far-reaching change has occurred in the father's experiences surrounding childbirth, one that promotes greater supportive involvement with the mother during labor and delivery and increased opportunity for direct experience with the young infant. Research has shown that the father's presence during labor and delivery often results in the mother's receiving less or no medication. In addition, both mothers and fathers report very positive feelings about the total birth experience. Indeed, some parents have described participative childbirth as a peak emotional experience that strongly reinforced a sense of family commitment. Moreover, participating in childbirth is likely to be a positive influence on the pattern of adaptation to parenthood. As an outgrowth of the prepared childbirth movement, *The Father Book*, oriented to the father's perspective, is a guide through the experiences of pregnancy, childbirth, and the early months beyond.

In the period when books on parenthood characteristically were addressed to mothers alone, most were, oddly enough, written by men. The tables are turned in this volume, for the authors are a consortium of six women. This aroused a degree of suspicion in me, for I wondered how well they had the capacity to see the world through men's eyes. Was this merely a preachy treatise, exhorting men to "get involved" with their children? My fears were allayed, however. In the pages I came to see a recurring theme of *relationships:* father with mother, parents with child. With special sensitivity to this idea, one of the authors' major contributions is a perspective on fatherhood that sees it embedded in a sense of family.

This is not a "how to" book; it is, instead, a book that attempts to plumb a father's feelings, ideas, and experiences during the transition to parenthood. Rather than prescribing a single course of involvement, *choices* are presented which outline alternative ways of addressing the father's own needs, those of his partner, and of the newborn infant. Most of all, I find the authors' contribution to be a skillful synthesis of personal experiences and scientific research that can inform, support, and challenge the expectant father in the course of the remarkable transistion to parenthood.

Frank A Pedersen, Ph.D.
Child and Family Research Branch
National Institute of Child Health
and Human Development

Acknowledgments

We express our appreciation to the many people who helped us in researching and preparing this book: Shelly Barr, Marvin I. Bash, Cathy Djenab, Mark Guyer, Jennifer Ayers, Julia Meek, and Elizabeth McGlone. We are grateful to John D. Grad for legal advice and for his assistance in drafting Appendix I and to Jan Shaffer for her work on the father-infant exercises. We are deeply indebted to Sidney Lutzin and Mike Katz for their guidance and interest in this project and to Al Hackl, Laurie Tag, and Sandy Trupp for their encouragement and assistance in the production of this book. A special thank you is reserved for our editor, Rhonda Heisler.

R.K.G., D.B.B., R.L.G., Z.O.A., M.A.S.T., D.McV.R.

INTRODUCTION

Becoming a Father-To-Be

Ask a little boy, "What are you going to be when you grow up?" and he might answer, "a doctor," "a lawyer," or "an Indian chief." Almost never will he answer, "a daddy." In our society boys are seldom reared to think of themselves as future fathers. And seldom do they spend their time playing at being daddies. Boys are socialized as males but frequently this socialization concentrates on male activities other than those involving the family. Thus, although the majority of American men do eventually become fathers, the father-to-be often finds himself with less than nine months to prepare for what will be a major role for the rest of his life.

Everybody appreciates that the nine months of pregnancy are, for the mother-to-be, packed with a mixture of excitement and anxiety. But who ever thinks about the father-to-be? What do those nine months mean to him?

You are a father-to-be. You already know that your condition is, in fact, as new and precarious as your partner's. You are likely to feel a great deal of turmoil in your life because your partner's pregnancy can affect you emotionally, intellectually, and sometimes even physically.

Your involvement in the pregnancy occurs on a number of levels. From the moment you announce your status as a father-to-be, your existing relationships, especially those with your partner and parents, acquire new dimensions. Some of the changes are very rewarding while others may be difficult and disturbing. You begin to consider the new relationship you will form with your child. If this is your first child, that relationship will be unlike anything you have experienced before. You may wonder how you will measure up as a father, how you will enjoy being a father, how successfully you will be able to juggle the demands of work and home life. You may even wonder whether having a child is what you really want.

On another level, you will probably feel concerned and anxious about the well-being of both your partner and your baby. Usually these feelings surface as soon as the physical evidence of your partner's pregnancy is manifest. When your partner is experiencing discomfort, you can commiserate with her and may be able to relieve some of her distress. When she is feeling fine, you can share in her pleasure. However, throughout the nine months, you are likely never to feel completely free of fears about the baby's condition. This kind of relief may be possible only after you have actually seen your baby with your own eyes.

During the pregnancy, you and your partner must consider a number of practical matters concerning the birth of your baby. You become, in common parlance, consumers in the birthing market. It is important to determine your rights and options and your obligations to others. You must choose the kind of birth experience you would like to have. And if you and your partner disagree over any of these decisions, you need to try to resolve the differences.

Thus, for both parents-to-be the pregnancy period is both enjoyable and troubling, a time of turmoil and of calm, of excitement and of anxiety. A prominent pediatrician, Dr. T. Berry Brazelton, has stated, "I now see the shakeup in pregnancy as readying the circuits for new attachments, as preparation for the many choices which [the parents] must be ready to make in a very short critical period, as a method of freeing their circuits for a kind of sensitivity to the infant and his or her requirements. . . . Thus, this very emotional turmoil of pregnancy and that in the neonatal period can be seen as a positive force. . . ."[1]

This book is for you, the father-to-be. Although the personal experience of pregnancy is unique for each father-to-be, there are certain facets of the experience each man shares with other men. The more information you can gather about what to expect and how you might feel, the easier it will be to make informed decisions and deal successfully with the events of the pregnancy period. The acquisition of specific information can enhance your intellectual and emotional flexibility, enabling you to handle events in a rapidly changing situation. The more informed you are about the pregnancy and about your own feelings, the better you will be able to communicate with your partner. And the more communication there is between the two of you, the greater your share of satisfaction and happiness in experiencing the birth of your child.

This book provides several types of information about birth, preparation for birth, and events after birth. Chapter One focuses on the decisions that you and your partner must make concerning the way in which you want your baby to be born. Chapters Two and Three discuss how your partner's pregnancy may affect the emotional, intellectual, physical, and sexual spheres of your life. In Chapter Four you will learn how other men have chosen their own levels of involvement in pregnancy and birth. Following a discussion of childbirth education in Chapter Five, Chapter Six describes the specific roles available to you if you have decided to coach your partner through labor and delivery. Chapters Seven and Nine cover the labor, delivery, and postpartum periods. The events that may disrupt a smooth pregnancy or birth are discussed in Chapter Eight. Chapters Ten and Eleven provide an introduction to life with a newborn. Finally, in Chapter Twelve, an overview of trends in fathering is presented.

The personal and professional experiences of the authors, reviews of the literature and person-to-person interviews with forty-seven men all figured in the writing of this book. Excerpts from these interviews are included throughout the book to illustrate significant issues.

If you are about to become a father, we hope this book will be of help to you. Good luck in your occupation as a father-to-be!

The Alliance for Perinatal Research and Services, Inc.
Rae Krohn Grad *Zoila Ortega Acevedo*
Deborah Blumenthal Bash *Mary Anne Staigers Trause*
Ruth Levy Guyer *Diane McVittie Reukauf*

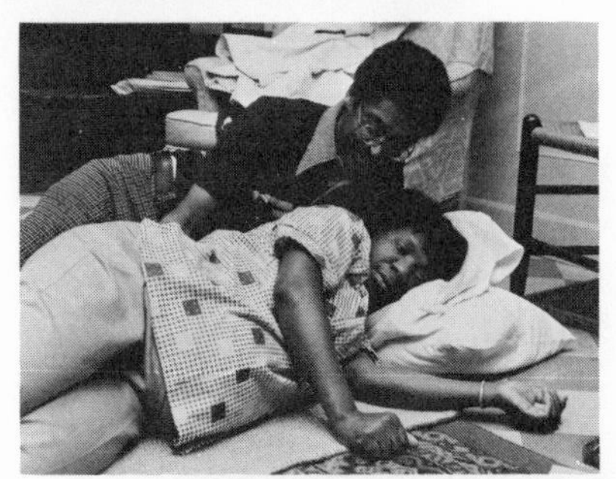

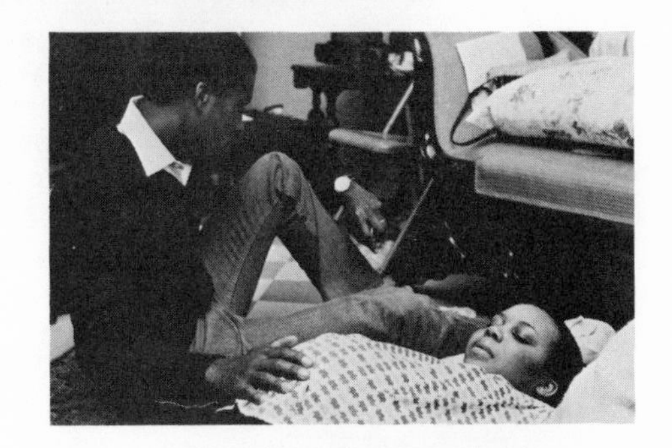

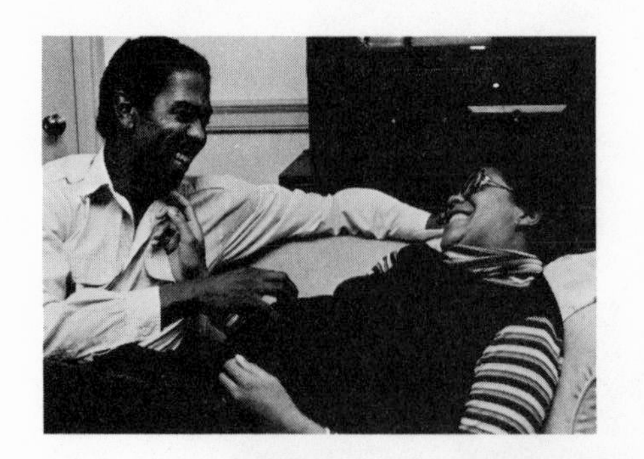

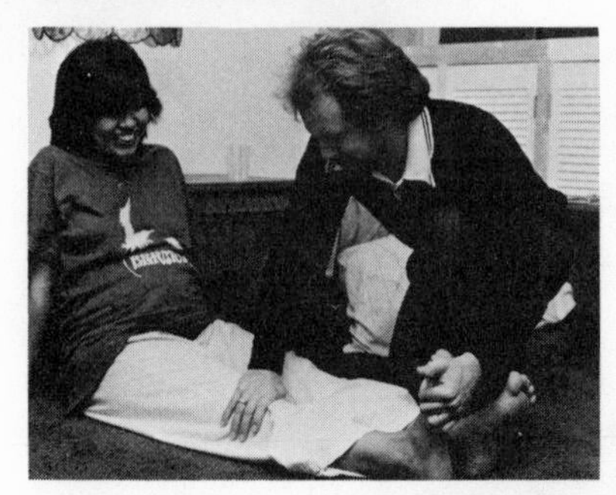

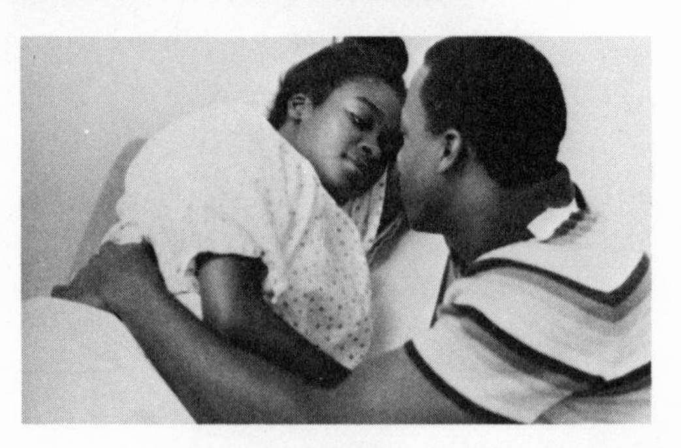

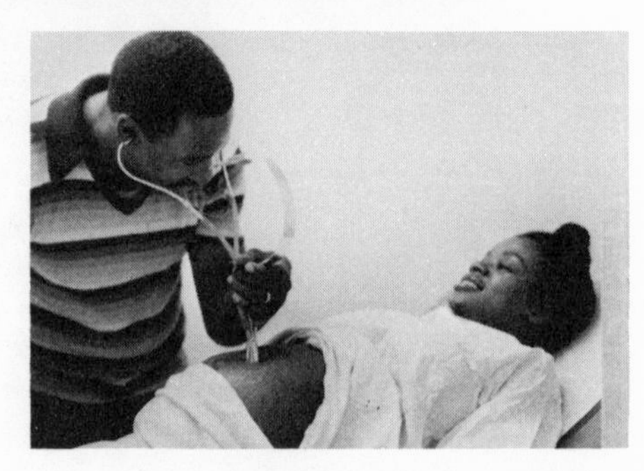

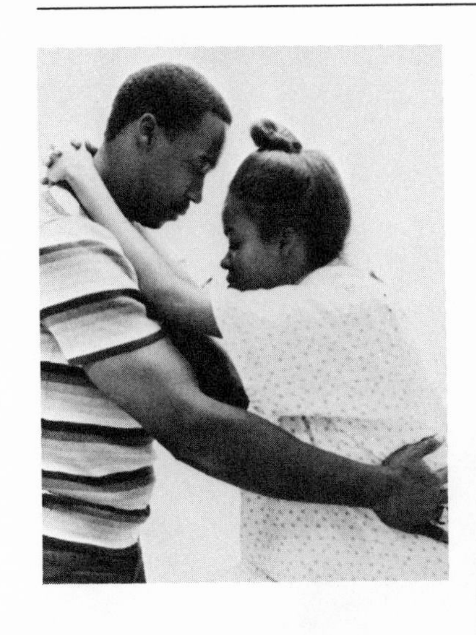
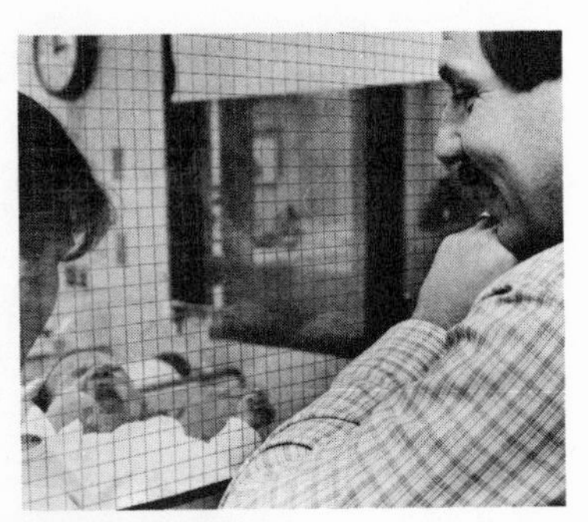
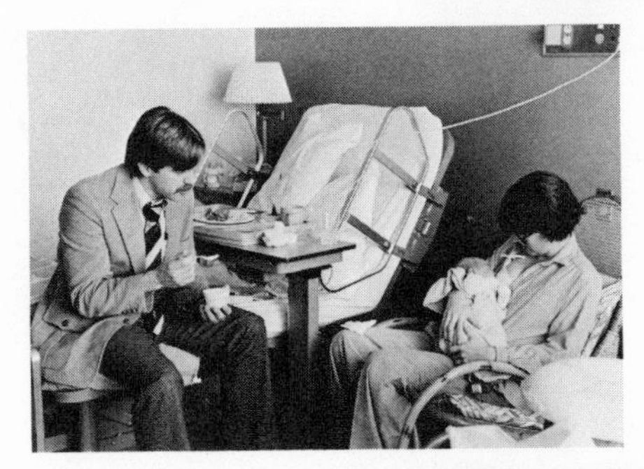
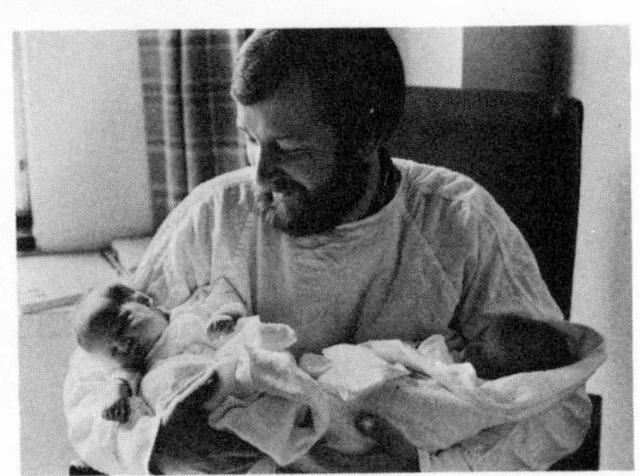

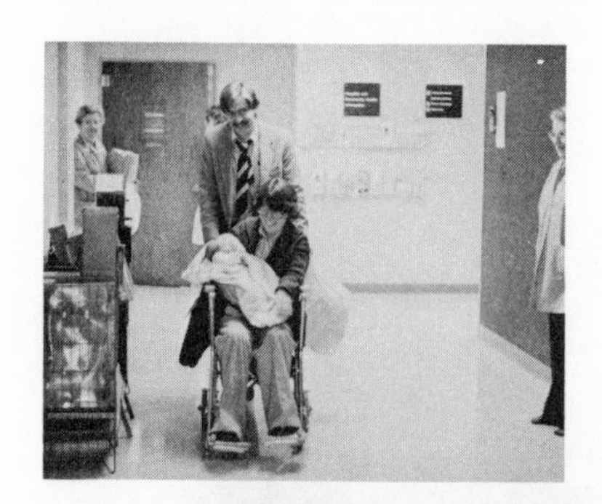

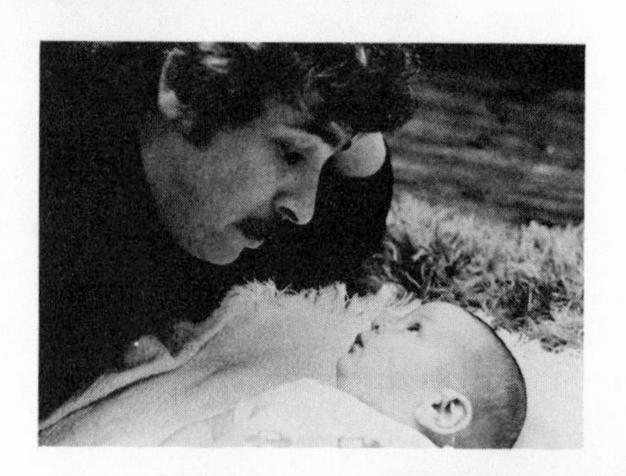

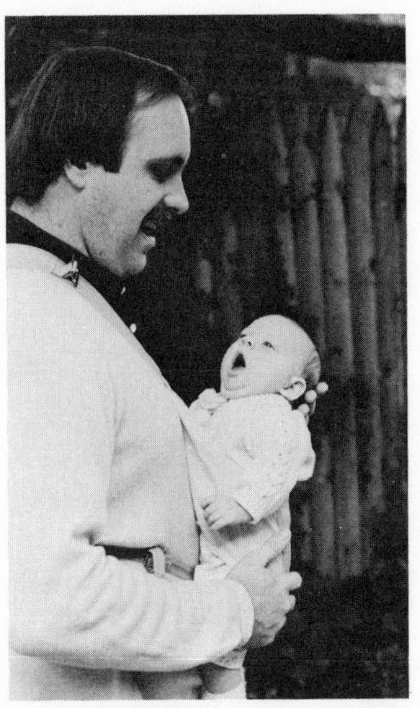
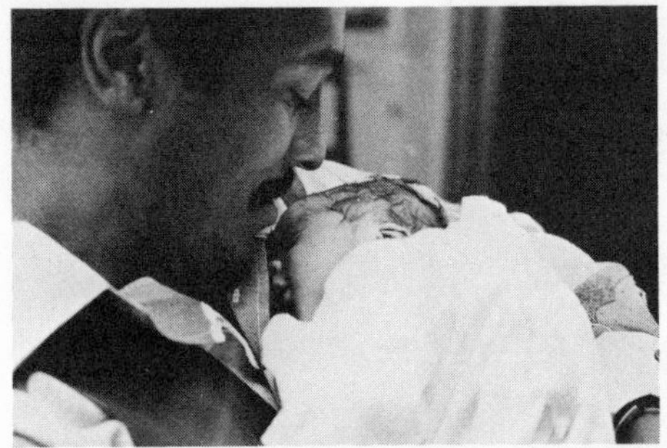

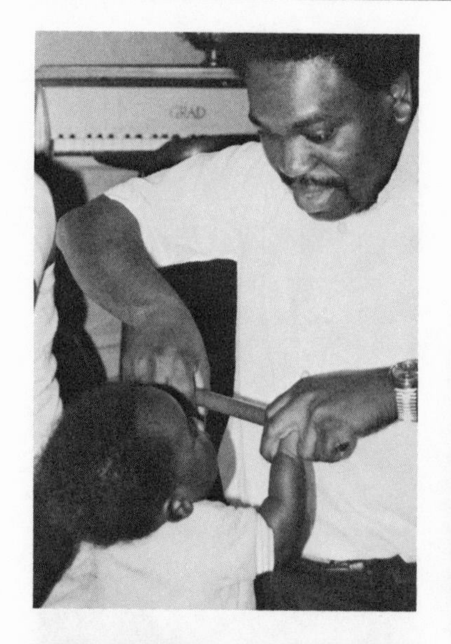

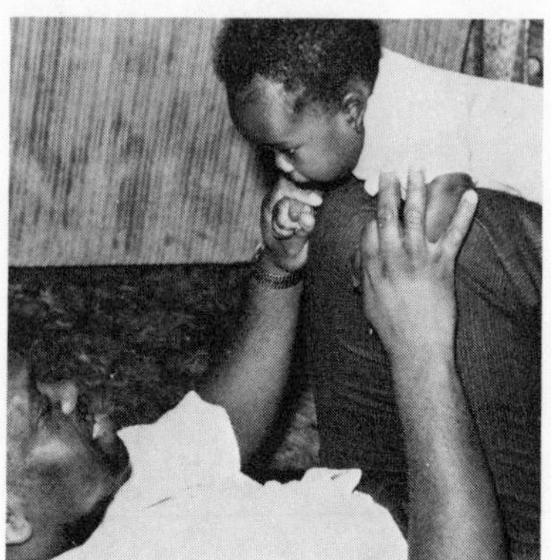

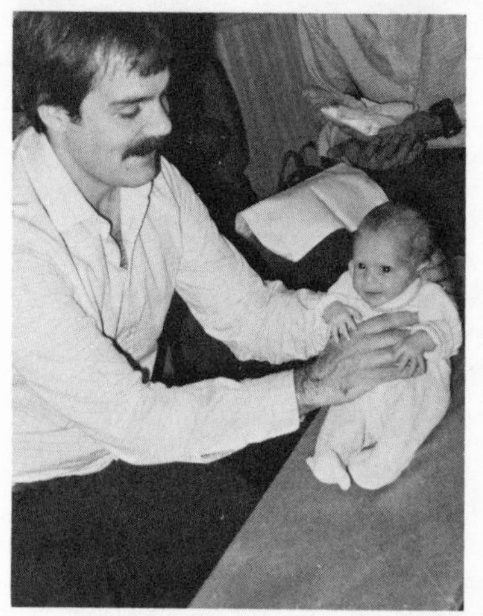

CHAPTER ONE

Preparing for the Baby's Birth: Making Choices

You are going to be a father. Whether or not this is your first time in this role, the mere prospect of becoming a father is likely to raise some questions in your mind and cause some dramatic changes in your life. Pregnancy is a time of self-discovery, exhilaration, excitement, anxiety, and change. At times you may feel unbelievably happy and content. Other times, you may find yourself yearning to return to the security of your prepregnant status.

Today, childbirth is not a package deal. There is no single right way to have a baby. Every father is different from every other, every mother is different from every other and, indeed, every baby is unique. As a consequence, each family has individualized needs. During the 265 to 280 days of pregnancy, you and your partner should be evaluating the options available to you so you can tailor the circumstances surrounding the birth of your baby to reflect your own needs and desires.

In trying to plan the ideal birth experience, most couples consider certain key issues—where to have the baby, who to include in the labor and birth, how much medical intervention is desirable, and so on. Sometimes decisions are based upon what is most convenient or what is economically feasible; other times decisions reflect strong convictions about social practices or medical procedures.

The time to begin discussing your preferences is early in the pregnancy. Investigate the options; talk to health care providers and to friends and relatives who have experienced pregnancy and childbirth. As you and your partner gather information, you will begin to form opinions about what is right for you.

Many couples shop for hospitals and doctors or midwives who can provide both safe and satisfying birth experiences. For some couples, the presence of the father during labor and birth is crucial, for others not. Some couples seek a hospital that allows sibling visits so that older children can visit mother and see the new baby. Other couples consider the availability of an intensive care nursery of highest priority in the event the baby has a medical problem. Couples differ in their feelings about various medications, fetal monitors, "prepping" procedures, and episiotomies. Some couples want to have their baby delivered at home to ensure a close, private time for the new family immediately after birth. Some parents want to use the birthing room of a hospital; some choose a maternity center. Some couples want a classic or modified Leboyer birth in which attempts are made to reduce the baby's presumed birth trauma.

As you and your partner plan the birth of your baby, here are some issues you may want to consider:

- How will you and your partner prepare for the birth so that the events that occur will not be unexpected? Will you attend childbirth classes (conducted by which organization?), have private instruction, read books and manuals?
- Where is the best place for your child to be born: at home, in a maternity center, in a hospital birthing room, or in a hospital delivery room?
- Will you personally participate in the birth or will you be absent? Does your partner want you to be with her during labor and/or birth? Do you want to be there? How can you resolve any differences you may have?
- Who is the appropriate health professional to attend the birth of your baby: a nurse-midwife, an obstetrician, a lay midwife, or you? If you alone will attend, by what health personnel will you be trained to assist in the birth? The birth attendant(s) you choose must meet your needs and your partner's needs and be willing to let you both do what you want within the bounds of responsible care.
- Who is the appropriate health professional to care for your baby: a pediatrician, a family or general practitioner, or a pediatric nurse practitioner? Have you made arrangements to talk with this practitioner before birth? Will this person visit your baby in the hospital or at home soon after birth?

- How do you and your partner feel about breastfeeding? If you are both in favor of it, how will you try to learn about it before birth? Do you know someone (or an organization) who can answer your questions about breastfeeding?
- What household help would be most valuable to you in the immediate postpartum period: your mother or mother-in-law, a domestic, a baby nurse, a special friend, or no one?

CHILDBIRTH PRACTICES: OLD VERSUS NEW

Childbirth practices are constantly evolving and changing. You should be aware that the most modern techniques are not always the best. Childbirth is, after all, a natural process for the female body. In some societies it occurs without any outside intervention. History has shown us that in some primitive cultures, childbirth practices were much more advanced than those that followed later. Over the years "civilization" has added new dimensions to birthing practices, some of which have been helpful and some of which have introduced complications.

For example, when women left their homes to have their babies in hospital wards, childbed fever became a serious problem. This infection was spread down the ward as each woman was examined internally by doctors who did not wash their hands between examinations. The maternal mortality rate that resulted from childbed fever was staggering, in some settings as high as 100 percent.[2]

Another dubious contribution was the introduction of the flat delivery table, a replacement for the horseshoe-shaped obstetric chair on which women used to sit during labor and delivery. The substitution was instituted by Louis XIV because he wanted to watch the birth of his children and found that the obstetric chair impaired his view.[3] Although the flat table made the birth easier for Louis, it meant that gravity could no longer play an active role in helping bring the baby down the birth canal. Today many hospitals recognize this factor and provide a wedge-shaped support under the head of the delivery table, thereby enabling the woman to be in a more upright position during labor and delivery.

General anesthesia was another "advance" that has now been largely abandoned. It became popular in 1853 when Queen Victoria asked for general anesthesia during childbirth.[4] It is now a well-known fact that drugs taken by pregnant women pass through the placenta and may have negative effects on the fetus. It is therefore important that the pregnant woman, both during her pregnancy and at the time of delivery, keep drug intake to an absolute minimum. (See Chapter Four for additional information on social and technological innovations in childbirth practices—some of which did not always aid in the process of birth.)

Of course, not all innovations were bad. Birth may have been a natural process, but it was not always a rosy experience for the primitive woman or even for women as late as fifty years ago. Many women died in childbirth of complications that might easily have been overcome by certain modern obstetric practices. Today health and normality are the norm for most families who take advantage of modern obstetric care, although defects and deaths have not been eliminated entirely. In the United States maternal mortality is about 14.5 per 100,000 live births;[5] in the 1920s the figure was thirty-three times higher.[6]

Figures for infant mortality are likewise encouraging. In 1976 the U.S. infant mortality rate was 15.1 per 1,000 live births.[7] About 8.6 per 1,000 live babies were born with congenital anomalies.[8] In 1977 about 80.8 per 1,000 live babies were born prematurely.[9] The concerned father should realize that tragedies can happen but should not be irrational in fearing for the health of his partner and baby (see Chapter Eight).

CHOOSING TO CHOOSE

The choices you and your partner make before and during her labor and delivery should be based on informed consideration of the benefits and risks of each option. Each father who discussed his ideas with us emphasized how different factors contributed to the decisions that he and his partner made. The following case history illustrates some of the difficulties encountered by a couple who did not give careful consideration to many of these issues until the birth of their second child.

Steve and Pamela: Attitudes Can Change

Steve and Pamela had their first child while they were in graduate school. Although having a baby at that time created an additional financial strain, Steve felt somewhat compensated by the fact that his flexible hours would allow him to become actively involved in child care. He looked forward to getting to know the baby well. Steve also had been impressed by childbirth documentaries he had seen on television and thought that taking part in the labor and birth would be an interesting experience. He decided that if he had the option, and if Pamela were interested, he would participate.

However, Pamela's obstetrician did not approve of fathers being present at birth. Because the doctor was a family friend and had a fine reputation, Steve and Pamela did not consider voicing their disagreement, especially since the obstetrician had agreed to charge them no more than the relatively meager maternity benefits provided by their insurance.

As it turned out, the birth was extremely difficult for Pamela. Steve was allowed to be present during much of the labor, and during that time Pamela was reassured by his presence. Eventually Steve was sent away. Pamela was given medication, and she became very frightened. Most of the nurses seemed competent and efficient, but she felt very little warmth or support from them. She knew her doctor better, but he seemed rushed and was present for only short periods of time. Pamela had a long labor and delivery. She was given a general anesthetic, and the baby was born while she was asleep. Her only recollection is of the recovery, which was confusing and scary.

Five years after this birth, Pamela and Steve had moved to a new town and were preparing for the birth of their second child. Neighbors recommended an obstetrician associated with a highly-rated hospital. Pamela suggested that she and Steve attend childbirth preparation classes as her new doctor had recommended. Steve agreed. He felt classes might help him learn how to be useful to Pamela in labor. He remembered vividly his feelings of helplessness and frustration when he had not known what to do or say. But the fright associated with Pamela's first delivery had squelched his desire to be present at the birth of their second baby. To Steve, childbirth seemed to be full of suffering, and he was afraid to witness Pamela in pain again. He did not admit these fears to Pamela. He simply told her that he felt he could help during labor and he would do that but felt that it was the doctor's job to help with the delivery. Pamela went along with his decision.

Steve felt that he was a good coach during Pamela's labor. He thought he was in touch with her needs and was able to help her relax and breathe using the techniques they had learned and practiced. He found the experience tremendously satisfying and worthwhile, although still a little frightening. The hospital staff made him feel at home and encouraged him to stay with Pamela after she received an epidural, an anesthetic that affects the pelvic area.

Even though the labor progressed smoothly, Steve did not accompany Pamela to the delivery room. Instead, he waited outside until just minutes after his new daughter's birth. Pamela was so elated about her experience that Steve says he would like to be present if they have a third child. He attributes his changed attitude to several factors: his increased confidence in his ability to provide real help to Pamela; Pamela's positive, happy experience; an obstetrician who had managed the birth in a competent, relaxed, and personable manner; and enlightened hospital policies that were strongly supportive of family-centered care.

As Steve and Pamela moved from their first childbirth to their second, they decided that some factors were too important to be decided by others, or worse, to be left to chance.

In reading this book, you will have an opportunity to consider the choices made by a number of the couples we interviewed. It is hoped that you will find some of this information useful in helping you make your own informed decisions. You may also be able to profit from the "mistakes" these couples felt they made. Remember, there is no one set of choices that is "correct" for every couple, for every pregnancy. There is only one unfortunate decision for any couple—and that is a nondecision.

As you begin to implement your plans, it is important to remember that as a father-to-be you have certain rights, some of which are summarized on the following page.

BILL OF RIGHTS FOR THE FATHER-TO-BE

As an expectant father you have the right to:

Determine what is best for you.

Make choices about the birth and have your choices acknowledged and respected.

Be a partner in the birth of your child, if you wish.

Not participate in the birth of your child, if you wish.

Insist on clarifications.

Make informed decisions.

Question medical personnel.

Question standard childbirth practices and policies.

Expect your dissatisfactions to be resolved through mutually acceptable compromises.

Receive treatment appropriate to an adult.

Hold and caress your child.

Express or withhold your feelings about the childbirth experience.

Protect your partner, your child, and yourself.

CHAPTER TWO

Your First Eight Months as a Father-to-Be

For the father-to-be, feelings of joy and excitement usually accompany the confirmation that a wanted baby has been conceived. In the case of an accidental or unwanted pregnancy, there are likely to be negative responses, such as anger, fear, guilt, disappointment, or ambivalence.

Soon after your initial reaction to the news of the pregnancy, you will no doubt experience a number of fears and concerns about the pregnancy, about the birth, and about life with baby. Will the pregnancy and birth go smoothly? Will the baby be all right? Will you be able to cope with any problems that arise? How successfully will you be able to handle the responsibility of a dependent child? Will you enjoy this responsibility? Will you enjoy being a father? Will more be gained or lost in your relationship with your partner once the baby has come? Will you be able to manage the increased financial burden? Every expectant father has a number of other worries to add to this list.

At times you might feel uncomfortable and anxious as you mull over these and other legitimate questions. And you may not know how to find help in dealing with your anxieties. Although a myriad of friends and family seem to offer support to your pregnant partner, you may find that for the most part you are ignored or treated as a person who is only marginally involved in the pregnancy. Others may seem uncaring or at least unaware that your activities and emotions are, like hers, somewhat disarranged by the pregnancy.

Take some comfort in the fact that you are not alone, either in your anxieties or in your feelings of isolation. Since your partner may be as beset by worries as you are, it might help you both to air these concerns and share them. Although you may be reluctant to add your own problems to hers, talking about your fears is likely to lessen some of them. In addition, you might find that this kind of discussion produces feelings of closeness between the two of you.

If you can, take your worries beyond the complaining stage by doing something practical. For example, if you have specific concerns about the health of your baby, do some research on your own or talk to your physician or midwife. If you are worried about finances, look into insurance plans or loans. If you are concerned that your partner may never regain her figure, consider all the shapely mothers you know. By thinking rationally and taking practical steps, you and your partner are likely to feel reassured and more relaxed.

Aside from your partner, the person most likely to be most sympathetic to these concerns is another father-to-be. If one of your acquaintances isn't sharing your pregnant father status, remember there are a lot of former fathers-to-be who still can remember the turmoil of their own partners' pregnancies. But perhaps you feel isolated not only in your anxieties but also in your feelings of joy. Friends and colleagues less interested than you in the details of pregnancy may assume a glazed expression when you bring up the subject of fatherhood for the fourth lunch hour in a row. Many fathers-to-be feel uneasy or embarrassed about appearing too soft or sentimental and try to contain their excitement.

CHANGES IN YOUR RELATIONSHIP WITH YOUR PARTNER

What is happening to your relationship with your partner? It is the rare couple for whom no change occurs. You may be feeling especially close, tender, and loving toward each other, and you may be finding new interests to share. At the same time, established patterns in your relationship may be undergoing dramatic reshuffling.

Most couples who live together share certain basics: meals, household responsibilities, leisure time, and a sexual relationship. You and your partner may have enjoyed starting each day together over breakfast; she may even have prepared it for you. But for a woman with morning sickness, eating breakfast, much less cooking it, may be out of the question. The aroma of food may be too much for her to stomach early in the morning.

Perhaps you have enjoyed an active nightlife together, spending many evenings at movies, restaurants, or dancing. But now your partner may have no energy at the end of the day. She may prefer to stay close to home and turn in early. How will you feel about changing some of these established patterns? Remember, every father-to-be has had to live through these kinds of adjustments. Maintain your equilibrium by talking to other fathers, by viewing films on fathering, or by reading a variety of books on the subject of fatherhood.[10]

You may feel confused and disappointed to discover that the partner you felt you understood and on whom you had grown to depend is no longer herself. In addition to this upheaval in your expectations of your partner, it is likely that she is now relying on you in new and different ways. Every pregnant couple has different needs and experiences different changes in the pattern of their lives. If the reordering of your relationship is to be successful and satisfying for both of you, there must be empathy on both sides. You will both need to understand and retain a sense of humor about the nuances of happiness, guilt, ecstasy, ambivalence, anticipation, and anxiety that accompany any pregnancy. You both have to accept, usually without question, the labile emotions typical of and beyond the control of most pregnant women.

Ben D. comments:

> *Sometimes I think we are both going "nuts." I used to look forward to coming home for a nice quiet dinner after work. Well, now I never know what is going to set Mimi off, what will turn a quiet evening into a night of tension and hostility. For instance, yesterday I called home during the afternoon to see how she was doing. I casually mentioned I would be home at six o'clock for dinner. I got held up at the office with phone calls and didn't get home until twenty after six. You would have thought I committed a major crime!*

She started to cry and said I was uncaring and didn't understand her. She sulked over dinner and gave me icy stares. Finally after a big crying spell she admitted that she was lonely during the day and scared of the upcoming birth. We talked and hugged long into the night and I really felt very close to her. I wanted to protect her. I feel I love her more than ever, but these roller coaster evenings are hard to get used to.

You also have to acknowledge and accept your partner's often uncomfortable physical changes, including dramatic distortions of body image. The pregnant father's empathy is often so great that he himself may experience some nausea during the first trimester, some swelling during the last trimester, and/or a changed body image and sleep disturbances throughout the pregnancy. Although these changes do not correlate with hormonal changes in a man, they do reflect the intense emotional changes he is feeling.

In any sound relationship there are times when one partner must give more than the other. Very often your pregnant partner may be less flexible than usual. You are likely to be more satisfied with yourself if you can be somewhat more accommodating toward her. This is why it is so important to become informed, remain flexible, and communicate with your partner. Remember, pregnancy does not last forever—although it may often seem that way. Your relationship with your partner will change again after your baby is born. While the relationship will never be exactly as it used to be, it probably would not have remained the same anyway. After all, change and growth characterize any healthy relationship.

Exercise your option to view the changes a child brings as positive, dynamic, and growth-producing. The strength and love that define the "old" relationship never die; they just move into a new dimension.

YOUR PARTNER'S PHYSICAL CHANGES

During the months of pregnancy an incredible amount of growth and development is going on inside your partner's uterus. That just two cells can unite and become the basis of a unique human being is truly awe inspiring. Awe, however, may not be the dominant feeling these changes will evoke in your partner. Instead, she is likely to feel some degree of physical discomfort. You may empathize with her to such an extent that you too may experience "sympathetic" discomforts. Here are some common problems she may experience and suggestions on how you can help her cope.

Morning Sickness

Morning sickness is a frequent accompaniment of early pregnancy. It can take many forms; some women feel sick only in the morning, some only in the evening, some all day, and some only at the sight of particular foods or at the smell of certain odors. Its cause is unknown, although it is now generally recognized to reflect fluctuating blood sugar levels. Some health professionals feel that it is hormonal; and others say it is psychological.

Regardless of when or how it occurs, morning sickness can be a problem for both partners. There are a number of things you can suggest and do to help your partner through the period of morning sickness. She may find it very helpful to have tea and crackers first thing in the morning before getting out of bed. It is often soothing to switch from a three-meal schedule to a routine that calls for eating several small snacks during the day. These small meals (half an apple, a few teaspoons of cottage cheese) help to maintain blood sugar at a fairly even level.

In rare cases, morning sickness progresses to a stage where your partner cannot keep anything in her stomach. This condition, called *hyperemesis gravidarum*, is serious and requires hospitalization.

Cravings

During pregnancy some women experience strong cravings for certain types of foods. Some women crave starchy foods; others yearn for oranges or other citrus fruits. During this period you might enjoy indulging some of your own food cravings as well. However, be careful not to let your partner's cravings and your own override her need for nutritious food. You may want to assent to a few midnight forays for pickles and ice cream but encourage her to make wholesome, nutritious foods the mainstay of her diet.

Sometimes cravings are manifest even in the face of nausea. Vic G. comments:

> *What a weird few months this has been. For the first few weeks after the pregnancy was confirmed Susan could not get out of bed for breakfast. I would bring her whatever she thought she could keep down. It was usually starchy stuff. . . oatmeal, toast, etc. One day she craved an English muffin. We had some old ones in the freezer and I quickly brought one upstairs to her. She took one look at it and started getting sick to her stomach. The muffins I had toasted were the kind with raisins in them, and looking at them must have really gotten to her. It seemed she could tolerate only really simple foods. Then one day the nausea went away and an appetite emerged. Fortunately her crav-*

ings were healthy ones. One night, though, she just had to have those little soft jelly candies. It was midnight, but I went to three stores trying to find them. When I finally got home, she was sound asleep! I don't mind all this business; the changes are kind of fun. . . and I got to eat the candies.

Enlarged Breasts

During the early months of pregnancy, your partner's breasts probably will become enlarged and tender. Be sensitive to this condition and exercise care in fondling or hugging to minimize her discomfort.

Urinary Frequency

This condition is common during the first months of pregnancy when hormone changes may influence urination, and again during the final months when the growing fetus presses on the bladder and reduces its storage capacity. There is not much you can do about this inconvenience except be understanding of the need to interrupt car trips and outings in order to locate a bathroom.

Loss of Energy and/or Motivation

Changes in energy and motivation levels are normal during pregnancy. The added excitement and anxiety that accompany pregnancy may even make you more tired than usual. Naps, early bedtimes, and more careful selection and scheduling of activities will help your partner conserve her energy. Most women are advised to continue whatever activities they traditionally enjoy, including ballet, swimming, tennis, and so on. However, pregnancy is not the best time to start a new physical activity.

ADJUSTMENTS IN SEXUAL INTIMACY

During and after the pregnancy, your sexual relationship with your partner is likely to undergo some changes. A good sexual relationship improves the love and respect a couple share. Until recently, health care providers usually bypassed discussions of sex during pregnancy, except for a polite, embarrassed suggestion that beginning around the eighth month of pregnancy, the pregnant couple should refrain from sexual intercourse until the six-week postpartum visit. This meant that couples traditionally refrained from sexual intercourse for a three-month period. Why? No one ever elaborated. Abstinence was just something recommended and observed.

Books that specifically address the issue of sex and sexuality during pregnancy maintain that lovemaking, which initiated the life of your unborn child, can be continued throughout pregnancy.[11] Of course, this does not mean that anything goes for every couple. You will both experience changes in sexual desire during the pregnancy period. These changes are normal. During the first trimester your partner may have decreased sexual needs and desires due to fatigue and nausea. You may even share a fear of harming the baby. This fear can be especially strong if you have had difficulty conceiving a child. Despite a flurry of news reports that suggest that intercourse can harm a fetus, there are no long-term, reliable studies that confirm this allegation. There is a great deal of pleasure and security to be gained from intimate relations during pregnancy, and this must be weighed against the concern that one or two banner headlines can cause.

During the second trimester, as you see that the pregnancy is being sustained, the situation becomes more relaxed. Both of you probably will experience increased sexual needs and desires. During the third trimester, however, your partner may be uncomfortable again, this time because of her size. And once again you both may fear for the baby's well-being. These concerns may limit or change the forms of sexual expression you choose.

The radical changes taking place in your partner's body—her enlarging abdomen and breasts, an increase in vaginal lubrication, and the miracle of your baby growing and moving there—may excite you or may clash with your image of a sexual partner. In all cases, your shared sexual activities must reflect your changing feelings, needs, thoughts, and fears about yourselves, each other, and the developing child.

Chapter Three enlarges this discussion of adjustments in sexual intimacy as it takes a close look at the physical and emotional changes that accompany the final month of pregnancy.

CHAPTER THREE

Your Ninth Month as a Father-To-Be

Whether you are expecting your first child or your fourth, the last few weeks of a pregnancy can seem to last an eternity. Because the baby is expected momentarily, you may hesitate to initiate new projects. On the other hand, the birth may still be six or eight weeks away, a rather long time to be holding your breath. The excitement and tension mount daily as you chart your whereabouts so that you can be reached at all times. Each night you park the car facing the hospital.

THE UPHEAVAL IN YOUR EMOTIONAL LIFE

You and your partner are not alone in feeling the developing excitement and anxiety. Hordes of well-meaning people begin to focus on the coming event. You probably will be asked repeatedly, "Isn't it time (or worse, past time) for Patricia to have her baby?" or "When are you going to become a father?"

Even if you are not ready to think constantly about the coming birth, everyone else seems to be thinking about it for you. Your mother-in-law may arrive two weeks before the expected date of delivery just to be there "in time." (To prepare yourself for your mother-in-law's visit, you may want to read an excellent discussion of the special problems you and she may face after the baby is born.[12] Discovering that you are not the first father to have these problems with a mother-in-law you simultaneously resent and appreciate may help you resolve any difficulties rapidly and successfully.)

Although you may have made careful plans so that the arrival of a baby nurse, a sister, or a mother-in-law would coincide with the arrival of the baby, plans sometimes go awry. No one could have warned you about the nurse breaking her leg, your sister developing pneumonia, or your mother-in-law being stuck in a snow storm. When making arrangements for help, avoid last-minute panic by preparing two or three contingency plans.

Some friends may try to help you feel comfortable, secure, and relaxed. However, it is not easy to remain calm in the face of all this attention. There is often one well-intentioned person who proceeds to tell the hair-raising story of his own experience at his child's birth. It is normal to feel annoyed or frightened when you hear reports of unusual childbirth experiences. Don't feel obligated to put up with such well-meaning but bothersome people. It is perfectly all right to feel a need for privacy and to act on this need. Not all fathers-to-be want to spend every waking hour talking "baby talk." Life continues to have other dimensions. Do what is right for yourself and your partner. Even the most annoying acquaintances are only acting out their need to demonstrate their concern and happiness and will most likely respect your needs and wishes.

As the due date approaches you may begin to have nightmares or "daymares" about the birth and about the prospect of being a father. Most parents-to-be report that both positive and negative subliminal feelings emerge at this time. These feelings are normal and common.

As your sense of family grows, you may find that you and your partner are drawing closer together. You might need to spend even more time with each other now to discuss your own feelings and make plans and decisions for the future. Try to be good listeners for one another. And strive to be sensitive to and tolerant of rapid shifts of mood. You will find that it is not easy to keep yourself and a pregnant woman happy in the last few weeks of pregnancy.

ADJUSTMENTS IN SEXUAL INTIMACY

Today fewer doctors and midwives discourage sexual relations during the last few weeks of pregnancy, provided that the woman has had no bleeding problems and the amniotic sac (bag of waters) is still intact. Once bleeding is observed or the sac ruptures, sexual intimacy should not include vaginal penetration.

Even without evidence of these physiological stop signals, some couples refrain from coitus during the last few weeks or days. Some couples are totally preoccupied with the business of preparing for the baby; others fear that sexual intercourse will initiate premature labor. This fear is not groundless. Male hormones in the ejaculate, female hormones released upon stimulation of the breasts or other erogenous zones, and the woman's orgasm (which causes slight contractions of the uterus) may induce labor or accelerate it.[13] In fact, as the due date approaches, some couples try to initiate labor in this way.

Even if you decide to refrain from coitus, you both will no doubt have a strong need for affection. Touching, fondling, massaging, relaxing with and talking to each other can be wonderfully satisfying ways to express love and achieve sexual gratification.

MORE PHYSICAL CHANGES YOUR PARTNER MAY EXPERIENCE

In the last weeks of pregnancy, your partner may develop new physical problems. Most of these are related to the bulk and position of the baby. Almost all of these problems go away as soon as delivery occurs. It is useful, however, for you to know about these conditions and be prepared for them. In some cases, there are specific things you can do to help her feel better.

Even minor problems can be emotionally trying for a woman who has spent the previous thirty-six weeks growing larger and larger and who, by the last month, is barely able to lumber through each day. The best way to relieve some of your partner's distress is to give her frequent opportunities to talk about her problems. Try to understand and sympathize with her ailments and her distress over them. Remember, by this time in the pregnancy, you and your partner have already waited ten times as long as you have left to wait before your baby's arrival.

Backache

Lower back pain is one of the most common discomforts that develops later in pregnancy. It is a result of the growing fetus pressing more and more on the mother's back which must support its weight. You might be able to ease your partner's backache by giving her a good massage. If you try massage, remember to start out with warm hands and warm lotion. Your partner may also find that certain exercises, such as pelvic rocking done on all fours, can alleviate back strain.

Sciatica

A pregnant woman can experience shooting pains down her leg when the baby presses on the sciatic nerve in the spine. This kind of pain is usually transitory and may be relieved by lying down on one's side.

Urinary Frequency

During the last month of pregnancy, the fetus seems to snuggle up against your partner's bladder. Most pregnant women make sure they know the location of every bathroom in their vicinity and may, in addition, urinate three or four times a night. Rather than decreasing her total fluid intake, your partner could perhaps cut back on the fluids ingested after 7 or 8 P.M. This will help minimize those nightly trips to the bathroom.

Leg Cramps

A leg cramp, or charley horse, can be quite frightening, especially if it occurs in the middle of the night. You can help your partner ease the cramp by bending her foot toward her face. The warmth of your hands around her leg will ease the pain. Do not attempt a vigorous massage of the cramped calf. It is a good idea to remind your partner to yawn and stretch with her feet flexed rather than pointed; pointed toes seem to set off a leg cramp.

Indigestion

Indigestion and/or heartburn can be a common complaint toward the end of the eighth month or at the beginning of the ninth month. Because of the baby's size and position, your partner's stomach capacity is limited. The opening into her stomach is relaxed. It's best to avoid huge meals and very spicy or greasy foods. It is also helpful to consume each meal in two parts so that the stomach has a smaller load of food to digest at any one time. For instance, she could eat half her breakfast at 8 A.M. and the other half at 10 A.M., half her lunch at 12 noon, the other half at 2 P.M., and so on. Discourage your partner from taking over-the-counter remedies for heartburn or indigestion without an okay from her health practitioner. In general, your partner should never take any medication without first consulting her physician or midwife. Some of the common stomach medicines contain large amounts of salt and it may not be advisable to take these during pregnancy.

Constipation

This problem can occur throughout pregnancy but is most common in the last month when already slowed digestion is further decelerated by the large size of the baby. Constipation can usually be resolved with a diet high in bulk food, fruits, vegetables, and water. Exercise can also promote efficient digestion and excretion.

Hemorrhoids

Hemorrhoids develop in conjunction with constipation or from the pressure of the baby. They can occur during pregnancy or after the baby is pushed down the birth canal. Ice packs and witch hazel compresses are probably the oldest and most beneficial remedies. Topical ointments can be purchased over the counter.

Shortness of Breath

Because the baby is pressing on the diaphragm and lungs, your partner may have difficulty catching her breath. There is not much she can do to alleviate this problem except to avoid overexertion.

Circulatory Changes

Poor blood circulation can cause edema (fluid retention) or swelling of the ankles, aching or throbbing of the legs, protruding blood vessels, and even varicose veins. You should remind your partner to rest periodically, propping up her feet to assist blood flow back to the heart. Maternity support hose or prescription support stockings are also helpful in forcing the blood back up the legs. Poor blood circulation to the brain, a result of standing still for a long period of time, may cause lightheadedness, although this can be alleviated by walking. When a pregnant woman lies flat on her back general circulation is also slowed, so you should always encourage your partner to rest on her side (preferably on the left side).

Insomnia

This is a problem that can plague both you and your partner. The physical discomforts of late pregnancy and worries about labor and birth can contribute to insomnia. Your insomnia may also reflect your partner's restlessness or her desire to talk to someone while she is wakeful. Ease her nights with a sense of humor and a lot of understanding. Hot milk, a late movie, a back rub, and cuddling are all effective and enjoyable countermeasures.

Lightening

There is one ninth-month physiological change (besides the baby's birth) that may make your partner feel better. Late in a first pregnancy, women usually experience a change called lightening or "dropping." Earlier in the pregnancy, as the fetus grows, it pushes the enlarging uterus up under the mother's breasts and exerts an uncomfortable pressure on the upper part of her body. With lightening, the pressure is relieved as the fetus settles down into the mother's pelvic cavity. Breathing, sleeping, and eating all become easier after lightening, though groin or leg cramps may soon follow.

As the ninth month drags on and the days and nights crawl by, you will find yourself wondering if the moment you've been preparing for will ever come. As Charlie K. comments:

> *The last month might as well have been a year long. It seems we "peaked" too soon. Our childbirth classes were over, the nursery was in order, the suitcase was packed. . . and we just waited. Ginny went ten days over her due date. Every day we would interpret each ache or pain as "this is it." We both felt hemmed in because we were reluctant to drive far from home or undertake a new project. Physically, Ginny felt fine except for the back and groin pain she experienced after the baby dropped. The doctors were very vague about her due date. One doctor said "any day now," and the other said "not quite yet." It's all a big guessing game anyway, since the baby comes when it is ready. . . not when we are. Everything was tense that last month. You know, we almost felt guilty in not producing the baby on time. We felt we were not living up to everyone's expectations.*

But every baby arrives eventually. One morning, afternoon, or evening you will get the signal for which you've been waiting these many weeks. Your partner will experience the unmistakable physical signs that labor is underway. Every aspect of the pregnancy period—the excitement, anxiety, exhilaration, and self-discovery—is about to be magnified in the drama and challenge of birth. Are you and your partner ready?

Before we describe what you are likely to experience in labor, delivery, and the postpartum period, we'd like to take a closer look at one of the most fundamental questions you face as a father-to-be: To what extent will you participate in your child's birth? Chapter Four considers those concerns that a certain number of fathers find limit their ability to participate. Chapter Five discusses how childbirth education classes prepare the pregnant couple for labor and delivery and train the willing father to perform a vital role in childbirth. In Chapter Six, five fathers who chose to participate tell what the experience was like.

Undoubtedly you will find your own attitudes and concerns mirrored in the personal experiences of one or more of these men. By reacting to their stories, you will be moving closer to deciding what your own special role will be.

CHAPTER FOUR

Father Participation: What Are the Issues?

When it comes to making arrangements for childbirth, one of the most common points of disagreement between a couple concerns the extent to which the father-to-be will participate in labor and birth. Today, in most communities, it is common for a man to participate actively in his partner's labor and his child's birth. Most men who have taken an active role report that the experience ranges from satisfying to exhilarating. Notwithstanding such rave reviews, for some men the prospect of being present during childbirth holds little or no appeal. It may even be objectionable.

It is important to realize that between these two extremes—full involvement versus no involvement—many couples have found satisfying compromises. Some men supported their partner's attempts to find a doctor or midwife whose approach to childbirth was compatible with her own. Others met the doctor or midwife during routine office visits and were given the chance to hear their baby's heartbeat. Some fathers who had no intention of participating in the labor or delivery process still attended childbirth preparation classes in order to become better informed. Others planned to assist their partners during labor, but not delivery.

How do you fit in? What will you do? If the decision of whether or not to be present at labor and birth is a difficult one for you, it is important that you try to articulate your own feelings about participating and find out how your partner honestly feels about your being there. It is hoped that you will be able to settle on an approach that you both find comfortable. In some cases, however, it will not be easy to reach a compromise. If you can discuss your views openly, perhaps you can at least come to respect these differences and agree to disagree. Refusal to talk about your feelings, especially if there are strong differences, could lead to resentment and tension between the two of you.

In the course of writing this book, we interviewed both expectant fathers and new fathers. Some of these men had decided not to participate fully in labor and delivery. As we listened to them, it became clear that their decisions had been based on serious consideration of issues pondered by many men contemplating participation in childbirth. We present some of their stories here in order to demonstrate these issues.

BIRTH AS A FEMALE AFFAIR

One couple we interviewed described their view of childbirth in historically traditional terms. Neither Alex nor Lisa had any desire to witness their child's birth. Both saw childbirth as intimately female and ultimately private. In Alex's words,

> *Lisa and I are very private people. It makes me feel uncomfortable to think that I could see her flat on her back on the delivery table, half undressed, in pain. I would feel like a voyeur. Besides, I don't want that picture of her to change my image of her as a lover. . . I just think that childbirth is the province of women. It's too private for men to observe.*

Alex explained that his only regret in not being with Lisa was the fact that he would have to wait outside the delivery area without knowing what was happening. He knew he would be nervously awaiting the news that his wife and baby were okay. Nonetheless, he felt that if a problem arose he would rather not be in the way. He had heard that childbirth often lasted much longer than fathers expected, so he planned to take sandwiches and some paperwork to the hospital to make the time pass.

Lisa expressed embarrassment at the prospect of having Alex present for her labor or for the birth of their child. In fact, Lisa felt embarrassed at the thought of having an unmedicated childbirth. She did not want to feel pain nor lose control. Lisa did not put much stock in the argument that the medication harmed the baby. Her own mother and the mothers of virtually all her friends were asleep during childbirth, and none of the offspring seemed to her to be adversely affected. Lisa shared Alex's view that natural childbirth was a fad. Lisa and Alex did decide, however, to attend their hospital's series of six childbirth classes in order to learn more about pregnancy, childbirth, and infant care, and to meet other couples who were having babies.

On the day Lisa's labor began, she called the obstetrician's office and was pleased to learn that the doctor she liked best was on duty. Once Alex and Lisa got to the hospital and had checked in at the admissions desk, Alex went to the father's waiting room. It was empty when he got there. He could not settle down to work so he got some coffee from a machine and turned on the television.

Alex said that after what seemed like hours, but what was only about forty-five minutes, a nurse came in to tell him that Lisa had been examined and was only in the early phase of her labor. If labor did not begin to progress, they could go home. Alex felt disappointed and hoped that this would not happen. He said he called a friend, then just watched television for the next couple of hours. When the nurse returned, she reported that labor was moving along and that the doctor had said Lisa should stay in the hospital. The nurse further explained that it would probably be many hours before the baby was born. Alex remembered reading, dozing, and watching the clock through the night. From time to time a nurse would appear to tell him that Lisa was doing fine. The night seemed to drag on and on.

At 6:37 A.M. Alex was led into the recovery room. Lisa said, "It's a girl!" and smiled as she looked from Alex to the baby lying next to her. Alex remembered his eyes filling with tears. "It was such an emotional thing, seeing Lisa and Julie together for the first time. I even remember crying and I don't cry very often. I was really glad that everything was okay."

Throughout history, men have played a relatively minor role in childbirth. This tradition is still the norm in many cultures. An examination of birth practices in contemporary nonindustrialized cultures reveals that over half do not allow male "doctors" to be present and even more exclude fathers.[14] Almost all provide female attendants who are usually the mother's older, more experienced kin.[15] Thus, in these societies birth is largely a female affair.

Until the beginning of modern obstetrics, around 1800, men were not involved in childbirth in any way, not even as medical specialists. In the early 1500s, a Hamburg physician named Dr. Werth wanted to see a delivery. He dressed as a midwife and sneaked into the room where the birth was about to occur. He was caught and, as punishment for his offense, he was burned at the stake.[16]

Oddly enough, it was Louis XIV who introduced men into the birthing process. One of his mistresses was about to give birth to his child. The king was curious and ordered his male court physician to attend her. He himself watched from behind a curtain. But when he found he could not see enough, he ordered his mistress's petticoats removed and had her moved from her birthing chair to a bed within his view. From that time on, the nobility, following their monarch's example, used beds for births and allowed male midwives, physicians, and surgeons into the delivery chambers.[17]

In the United States it is only within the last two decades that the expectant father has been encouraged to be present at childbirth. Many hospitals still exclude fathers. Even in hospitals where fathers are allowed to be present for labor and birth, men sometimes get the feeling that their presence is merely tolerated. Labor rooms may not be equipped with a comfortable chair for the coach, and there may not be a men's room in the entire labor-delivery area. Cafeterias are usually closed and food machines are empty through the long night hours when fathers might need a snack to keep them going. Nurses and doctors often ask the father to leave when his partner is being examined, giving the impression that fathers are in the way when there is serious work to be done. Barely a handful of hospitals allow fathers to stay for cesarean births.

On the other hand, the personnel in some hospitals are now actively welcoming fathers. Some doctors and midwives prefer to attend childbirths with prepared couples, claiming that such men and women know how to cooperate with the natural process, making everyone's "job" easier. Many nurses assist and support the men in their coaching role. The men we spoke to described the help they received in the following ways:

> *"The nurse got a chair for me because she said I'd been standing too long." . . . "I wasn't sure where to apply counterpressure when Mary said her back hurt, so the nurse found the right place and marked it for me with her pen." . . . "The doctor was great. He explained everything to me as we went along." . . . "Just before we went into the delivery room, one of the nurses gave me some orange juice. She said it would be good for my blood sugar. I was surprised anyone would be thinking about me."*

There are even some hospitals in the United States that provide a special celebration dinner for the new parents after the birth. Such trends indicate that fathers *are* beginning to be considered an important part of the birth process.

PRIVACY AND MODESTY

For Alex and Lisa the issues of privacy and modesty were important, compelling considerations. A look at other societies shows that cultures vary in their customs regarding privacy and childbirth. Not only is the woman giving birth often secluded from men, in some cultures she is even isolated from other women. In the Talamancan tribe in South America she delivers completely alone, even if there are complications. At the other extreme, birth is sometimes a community affair. Among the Navajo tribes, all who pass by, both men and women, are expected to come in and offer encouragement and moral support.[18] Within our own culture, individual couples' attitudes toward privacy also vary. For some couples the presence of *any* extra persons is an intrusion into the woman's privacy. But it is common among many who give birth at home to make the event a genuine celebration by having friends attend. Some families encourage older children to witness the birth of their new sibling.

For centuries the issue of modesty in childbirth had been a major one. Once men as medical specialists were permitted into the birth chamber, female birth attendants were gradually excluded. It was probably partially through this transformation that birth took on the additional problem of modesty; "it became a social event that challenged codes of purity and privacy."[19] Modesty required careful procedures on the part of any male-midwife or male birth attendant.

In the sixteenth century a French doctor, Ambroise Pare, operated with the women completely covered by linen cloths so that he could feel but not see what he was doing. . . . The Chamberlen family male-midwives kept their forceps a secret for three generations by

> *covering themselves and the woman's body with a sheet and working in the dark. [William] Smellie disguised himself as a woman. . . so as not to alarm his patients with a man's presence. Some eighteenth-century doctors tied a cloth about their necks and draped it over their hands and lower bodies, thus separating themselves visually from their actions.*[20]

So serious were the requirements of modesty that it was not until the second half of the nineteenth century that students of obstetrics were allowed to witness deliveries. Until then, "birth specialists" relied entirely on books for their training.

Today's hospital routines provide little or no opportunity for a laboring woman to be modest. Perhaps our advances in the science of obstetrics have brought us to a state where more weight is given to the execution of procedures than to the woman's emotional needs. Even a woman who values her modesty very highly is likely to be more concerned with giving birth to a healthy baby than with her desire to remain modest. This is not to say that a woman will easily abandon her personal standards of decency, but rather that she recognizes the difficulty or impossibility of worrying about certain details while involved in the important task of giving birth. Many mothers now report that, of necessity, they shed all modesty once they enter a hospital for childbirth. How can a woman be modest when she is dressed in a short open gown that is almost impossible to hold closed? Or while she is being observed by medical students? One childbirth educator told a class of Amish women, "It's good to lose modesty in the hospital. You must not be ashamed of your position in labor. . . . You can be modest again after you leave the hospital."[21]

Like Alex, the father-to-be often shares his partner's discomfort at the imposed immodesty. He may react to this by distancing himself from the experience, viewing the male doctor as a sort of medical machine, avoiding all communication with the male obstetrician. Women, too, will often avoid choosing a doctor whom they know socially or know as a professional colleague.

An unfortunate consequence of this awkwardness is that some men avoid meeting the obstetrician and discussing their concerns. Therefore, significant issues related to the birth might not be aired. For example, Alex and Lisa's notion that medication is not a hazard to the fetus is incorrect (see the sections in Chapters Five, Six, and Seven for a discussion of effects of medication). Even a man who chooses not be be present during labor and birth should discuss philosophies and practices of childbirth with the person who will help to deliver his baby so that choices can be based on accurate information.

CHILDBIRTH AND PAIN

A number of men who spoke to us described their worries that labor and delivery would be intensely painful for their partners. Some said flatly that they didn't feel up to witnessing such a trauma, especially because they felt there was nothing they could do to alleviate the discomfort.

Certainly these factors played a part in Ed's decision not to be present when his wife Laura gave birth to their sixth child. Ed had not participated in any of the children's births. At the time of the first pregnancy, almost thirteen years ago, fathers were not permitted in the hospital delivery room. Because the nearest obstetrician was thirty miles away,

Laura's doctor had been a local general practitioner who had no use for "this radical Lamaze business."

Laura described her first labor and delivery as a nightmare. There were no complications, but she was completely uneducated about what to expect and didn't know how she might cooperate with her labor and in the birth. The doctor offered no support. "I was a real act with Christopher's birth," she remembered. "I was terrified. I screamed and carried on. Ed heard much of it. I guess that was his introduction to childbirth."

There were serious complications with Laura's third pregnancy and the daughter who was born prematurely died within days. It was during the next pregnancy that Laura asked Ed to attend childbirth preparation classes so he could be with her for the delivery. Ed refused. He didn't even want to discuss the issue. The story was the same for each subsequent birth—Laura requested. . . Ed refused.

Ed felt strongly that labor and delivery are "medical things" and that he was not trained to be effective in anything medical. "I'm not qualified," he insisted. "I'd feel helpless." He reported that he spent about thirty minutes in the labor room on two different occasions and this further convinced him that the whole process is difficult and painful. "Laura didn't scream or cry, but I could tell she was in a lot of pain. I know she thinks that my being there would be helpful to her, but I'd be so emotionally involved I'd probably screw things up. I don't feel I could be a comfort because I'd be too uncomfortable."

Ed's discussion of labor and delivery was filled with the conviction that the experience *must* be a painful one for women. He could not believe the pain could be diminished by his presence. Certainly this conviction is in keeping with the religious education many receive. The Bible describes the disobedience of Adam and Eve, and tells of the punishments God decreed. "Unto the woman He said, 'I will greatly multiply they pain and thy travail, in pain thou shalt bring forth children. . ." (Genesis 3:16). However, some theologians now argue that "in hard work" or "in labor" might have been a more accurate translation of this passage.

Margaret Mead has suggested that when birth is not experienced, notions of its pain are intensified.

> *In societies where men have never been allowed to witness childbirth, their fantasies about its terrible nature may be unbounded. Arapesh men give pantomimed accounts of childbirth in which women are conceived as screaming in agony, whereas in actuality the women of the tribe give birth quietly and matter-of-factly, in difficult and uncomfortable circumstances, on the damp ground of a steep slope, in the dark, with no one to help except one other woman. . . The contrast between men's nightmares and the actuality is striking.*[22]

Ed probably would have profited from attending childbirth preparation classes even if he remained adamant in not wanting to assist Laura during labor and birth. His ignorance of the birth process increased his anxiety about the pain of labor and his own helplessness in the face of it. There is evidence that when women know what to expect in labor, their experience of pain actually decreases. Being supported by a prepared coach also reduces the experience of pain and increases the satisfaction women feel in childbirth. Thus pain is not a given. Its perception is influenced by knowledge, by preparation (including being physically fit and knowing how to relax), and by the presence of a trained, supportive coach.

In childbirth preparation classes, the birth process is broken down into manageable segments. Labor is divided into three phases (early, active, and transition), with each phase consisting of contractions separated by periods of rest. You and your partner learn what to expect in each phase and even learn the characteristics of each contraction—how long it lasts and when it is strongest. So in a sense you learn to manage labor by dealing with it one contraction at a time. You both learn breathing and relaxation techniques that will get you through each contraction. Once you have learned and practiced these techniques together, you will not be helpless. In fact, women say over and over again that they could not have managed their labors successfully without their coaches. Your help can be indispensable.

THE PROBLEM OF ROLE EXPECTATIONS

Michael and Pat both felt comfortable with their division of parenting responsibilities. They both saw infant care as primarily Pat's domain. Michael considered himself to be her moral support, providing the financial and emotional resources and security for her to manage the household. He considered himself an active participant in his children's lives, though not in their births.

Pat had been medicated and without Michael for their first two children's births. When she became pregnant for the third time, she wanted to prepare for a Lamaze birth. The idea of being present during Pat's labor and their baby's birth was very remote to Michael. He viewed his role as being in the local tavern announcing to the world that their child was about to be born. "After all," he commented, "who can you tell if you're in the delivery room?" Actually his attitude is more positive than our cultural stereotype of the expectant father. We typically portray him as "the lovable buffoon roaring in panic to the hospital with his laboring partner at ninety miles an hour, the chain smoking wretch pacing the waiting room, and the self-conscious bumbler fumbling out the cigars."[23]

Michael also felt that his job—he held a high-level position with an international relief agency—made it impossible for him to plan to be with Pat at a specific time. He was frequently called out of town on short notice to establish emergency relief operations after a major catastrophe. He had even missed his brother's funeral because he could not get a flight out of an earthquake-ravaged South American country where he was on an assignment.

Pat said she knew Michael so well she could have predicted he would not want to coach her during childbirth. She respected his feelings and didn't try to persuade him to change his mind.

She knew herself as well. Pat did not see childbirth as particularly romantic and didn't feel the need to share it with Michael. She had wanted to have a prepared childbirth in order to avoid medication and the subsequent grogginess she had experienced in her two previous deliveries. She wondered how labor would be when she knew what to expect. She was also eager to see and hold the baby immediately.

Since Pat's reasons for wanting a prepared childbirth did not revolve around her need to share the experience with Michael, she agreed to his suggestion that she find someone who could be a more dependable coach. Pat asked a longstanding family friend to attend classes with her and assist her in labor and birth. The friend—a woman with older children—was thrilled with this opportunity to experience vicariously what she too had missed. Her enthusiasm, her interest in the classes, and her ability to identify with Pat's feelings made her a sensitive, effective coach.

Until recently, fathers in our society have not really had any defined role during childbirth. This is probably an outgrowth of the crosscultural belief that birth is a female affair, with the father typically ignored, sent to a hunting or drinking party, or given some obscure tribal or religious function far away from his laboring partner. Once American childbirth was moved from the home to the hospital, any tasks earlier relegated to the father—such as fetching the doctor or boiling rags—became obsolete. One of the chief benefits of the prepared childbirth movement has been the recognition of the crucial role that fathers can play during birth.

There is yet another side to the question of role expectations, one that relates to how rigidly the couple defines the "male" and "female" roles in their relationship. The childbirth process puts some couples in an unfamiliar relationship with respect to one another. It is the woman's time to show how physically strong and competent she is, and the man is asked to provide emotional support and other "behind the scenes" comforts that the woman traditionally provides. The man cannot make her strenuous task "go away," and he cannot choose to bear the difficulty for her. For some couples this may be an unacceptable reversal of roles. Some men cannot tolerate functioning in a "feminine" supportive role, because such an arrangement may promote feelings of helplessness and impotence. If you foresee that this issue might cause problems for you, talk it over with your partner.

Finally, on the question of role expectations, some of the men we spoke to admitted that for them, their inability to participate fully in labor and birth was firmly linked to their inability to sort out their feelings about the prospect of parenthood. Concerns about being a father and the responsibility involved crossed the minds of most of these men during pregnancy. These included fears about holding, feeding, and taking care of a newborn. Expectant fathers often mentioned that they worried about hurting a small baby through clumsiness or ignorance. Some men worried that they did not enjoy their friends' children and hoped they would feel differently about their own. They wondered how they would feel about changes in their own activities, and they wondered, too, if their relationship with their partner would change.

In this regard, men reported that during the pregnancy they sometimes felt uncertain about whether they were providing enough emotional support and understanding. Consequently, they worried about their ability to be supportive after the baby was born. They also wondered whether they would get enough love and attention once the woman had to meet the baby's demands. Many wondered how their sexual relationship would change, especially since so many changes had already occurred during pregnancy.[24] Occasionally a man also voiced concern over what kind of mother his partner would be: would she be able to respond to the initial demands of motherhood and cope with the day-to-day turmoil?[25]

Your susceptibility to these fears during pregnancy underscores your own emotional investment in the process of becoming a father. In a sense, you are doing the spadework in preparation for becoming emotionally involved with your baby. You are readying yourself to be a father.

CHILDBIRTH AND TABOO

When Susan asked Tom if he would attend childbirth preparation classes with her and be present during labor and birth, he said he would rather not. He didn't change his mind even after hearing his brother-in-law's glowing account of his participation in the birth of his twins. Tom commented, "I didn't tell Susan that the idea of blood bothered me, but I did mention I was afraid of fainting. I was afraid I would be so nervous that I would make the birth more difficult for her. And if something did go wrong, what if I couldn't do anything to help? My presence would make it worse. A man wants to be left out of this sort of thing."

As the pregnancy continued, Tom found himself becoming increasingly nervous. Although Susan had no physical complaints and seemed to be relaxed and confident, Tom said he was terribly frightened that something would happen to Susan or the child. He did not discuss his fears with anyone, but they lingered at the back of his mind.

Afterwards, laughing at himself, he said, "You know what a bundle of nerves I was? When Susan started having contractions, I couldn't drive her to the hospital. Instead I took her to the fire station so the firemen could take her in their ambulance."

Tom did stay with Susan through labor, which lasted a short four hours. He comforted her by rubbing her back and talking to her. When the doctor transferred Susan to the delivery room and invited Tom to come, he said, "No thanks," but asked to be called in as soon as the baby was born. He remembered feeling a little guilty because he knew Susan was disappointed.

Immediately after the birth, Tom was called into the delivery room. He found Susan crying with joy, "It's a boy! It's a boy!" Only then as he saw for himself that Susan and the baby were okay, did Tom feel the wonder and awe of childbirth itself. Along with a rush of relief, he felt a twinge of regret that he had not seen his son born. But later, when he heard that the doctor could not hear the fetal heartbeat for several seconds, he was relieved not to have been there. "I think my own heart would have stopped," he said.

The worry Tom expressed about observing blood was mentioned by many other men. Our queasiness about blood, which is perceived as a central and aversive aspect of birth, has been attributed in part to the once prevalent superstition that menstrual blood was a "fatal poison" capable of harming a woman's mate, family, and the entire community if she did not leave the area for a period of time to undergo a purifying ritual. The Old Testament clearly relates the blood of childbirth to menstrual blood and provides regulations for the woman:

> *When a baby boy is born, the mother shall be unclean for seven days, with the same uncleanness as at her menstrual period. . . and then she shall spend thirty-three days more in becoming purified of her blood; she shall not touch anything sacred nor enter the sanctuary till the days of her purification are fulfilled. If she gives birth to a girl, for fourteen days she shall be unclean as at her menstruation, after which she shall spend sixty-six days in becoming purified of her blood.* (Leviticus 12:2, 4, 5)

Thus, the Mosaic law required that women undergo purification after giving birth. This ritual is still followed by Orthodox Jewish women. Among other religious groups "Women were not required to be cleansed after childbirth, but a visit to church was encouraged, to give thanks to God for the child. This euphemistic ceremony, the 'churching' of women, still continues, in Anglican, and other Protestant communities as well."[26]

The taboo regarding women after childbirth is prevalent in other cultures as well. After delivery, a Hindu woman is considered impure and untouchable for sixty days. She may not have contact with her family, her hearth, or her cooking utensils. In Africa, Nandi women are considered unclean for six months after giving birth. Some peoples also believe that the child is somehow contaminated by the blood of birth: among the Bantu, the father may not touch his child for three months after the birth.[27]

Some fathers we spoke to suggested that beyond the issue of the blood itself, they did think about uncleanliness when they considered attending a childbirth. Certainly there is much religious and cultural support for such feelings. Even the original move from home births to hospital births carried with it the suggestion that "going there saved contaminating one's own home with the soils of birth." It was "an impure. . . affair that happened best elsewhere."[28]

FEAR OF COMPLICATIONS

There is another kind of fear that operates to make certain men apprehensive about participating in childbirth—the idea that complications might arise. Some men fear a specific catastrophe—the death of their wife or the birth of a defective baby. Others just have a vague feeling that something will go wrong.[29]

This notion that birth is dangerous stems partly from the fact that childbirth was once closely associated with death. As recently as 1920 the number of mothers who died in childbirth was thirty-three times what it was in the 1970s.[30] The expectant father's concern is reinforced by the fact that most births occur in hospitals, traditionally places for the sick and dying. The panoply of equipment that is now part of the drama of a hospital birth—the I.V.s and fetal monitors—clearly conveys the notion that something may go wrong at any moment. It is easy to see why some people associate pregnancy and birth with sickness and danger, despite current trends to treat birth as a normal physiological event.

FATHER-NEWBORN INTERACTION

While Tom was not present for his son's birth, it is likely that both father and child benefited from their early contact with one another. Recent research on how parents become attached to their infants suggests that the minutes and hours immediately following birth may be the optimal time for "bonding" between the parents and infant to occur. This is partly attributed to the excitement parents feel when they finally get to see the baby they have been anticipating for so long. Many parents are especially ready to "take in" their baby at that time. Most babies are very alert immediately after birth, which makes them particularly appealing and able to captivate their eager parents. Many babies are able to look right at their parents and watch their faces as they move. They are likely to root actively toward the breast and suck strongly.

Just a short time later, the baby is likely to fall into a deep sleep to recover from the shock of birth. If parents first meet their infant when the initial period of alertness has passed, they will meet a sleepy creature who can barely be roused, much less look at them alertly. Seeing a baby's eyes open has been found to be especially powerful in eliciting nurturant feelings in parents.

Most of the research on bonding has involved mothers and their babies. Only two studies have focused on fathers. Both of these studies suggest that for fathers, too, contact with the baby immediately after birth has a powerful impact. In one study, fathers described themselves as totally engrossed with their newborns when they had this early contact.[31] In the other study, fathers who established eye-to-eye contact with their babies for one hour in the first three days after birth, and who undressed them a couple of times, were found to be more involved in the infant's care through the first three months of life.[32] The impact of these early bonding experiences is thought to extend beyond the newborn period, to affect the father-child relationship in later years.

"We're beginning to find more and more substantial evidence that the way in which we give birth affects our lives, the way we mother and father. The opposite of bonding between parent and child is not just nonattachment, it's alienation. Thus far, our [American] way of birth—separating mother, father, and child—has been consistent with our way of life."[33] No one can deny there has been a general weakening of close family ties among many Americans. This has been partially ascribed to the fact that important events like birth and death have been taken away from the family and now occur in hospitals. The customs that once surrounded these critical events served to bring the family together and strengthen its unity. The bonding studies suggest one possible way to reverse this pattern of alienation: to renew and strengthen family ties through shared births. Many fathers have commented on how their close cooperation with their partners during pregnancy and/or childbirth played a crucial role in strengthening their relationship.

It is important, however, not to simplify the concept of bonding. Seeing a baby born, or having contact with that baby soon after birth, does not ensure instant love and devotion. The research suggests that early contact helps the parent-infant relationship get started. It is not, however, either necessary or sufficient for a positive, lasting relationship.

Some people tend to assume that fathers are less interested, less nurturant, and less competent with infants than are mothers. However, research has shown that these assumptions are simply not true. Fathers are capable of caring for their newborns, and fathers and babies can share delightfully engaging interactions with one another. Most important, fathers have been found to develop intimate relationships with their newborns *even if they were not participants in childbirth.* Both crosscultural studies and studies of American men have shown there is no relationship between paternal participation in childbirth and later involvement with the child.[34]

Relationships need time and attention to develop. The parent-infant relationship is essential both to the survival of our infants and the species. It would be simplistic to assert that its ultimate success depends on a specific contact in this early, very limited time span. The moments following birth merely provide the first of many opportunities for the father and child to become attached.

The stories of these four men—Alex, Tom, Ed, and Michael—have suggested a few of the ways individual couples have chosen to manage their childbirths. For each couple, the particular solution was less important than the ultimate goal that a healthy baby be born to nurturant parents.

The choices involved in childbirth are but one aspect of your role as a parent. However, these decisions are important ones, having implications for the health of the mother and child and the relationship of family members. So you and your partner should study your options and weigh them in light of your individual wishes and needs. If you disagree, the best compromise might involve a decision like Michael's and Pat's to have an interested third person actively participate. Recognizing that choices may be limited by the influence of religion, culture, and environment, your decisions need to be made carefully and conscientiously.

Whatever plans you finally decide upon, accept the fact that they may not seem perfect or turn out just the way you want. And then, regardless of your role during your baby's birth, concentrate on the truly important task of being a father.

CHAPTER FIVE

Childbirth Classes

As expectant parents, one of the wisest decisions you and your partner can make is the decision to attend childbirth education classes. Although these classes usually begin late in the pregnancy, they focus on much more than just the events of labor and birth. The classes offer many types of support to pregnant couples, including:[35]

- information about the normal process of pregnancy, in order to reduce or eliminate physical and emotional discomfort throughout pregnancy
- accurate nutritional information
- information about breastfeeding and preparation of the breasts during pregnancy

- an environment that allows couples to discuss feelings and attitudes about pregnancy and childbirth
- instruction in breathing and relaxation techniques that will enable the mother to participate in the process of labor with a minimal need for drugs
- preparation for the father who wishes to participate in the birth of his child
- information about living with a new baby, including possible changes in attitudes and lifestyles.

Some fathers have commented that they resisted going to classes because they saw these classes as part of a conspiracy to manipulate them into being present during childbirth. These feelings of being manipulated are not always just fantasies. In fact, some doctors and instructors suggest that the best way to influence a reluctant father is to "get him to the first class." This reasoning presumes that he will be so captivated that he will be eager to participate in the birth. Many less-than-enthusiastic fathers do report that their interest in participating is heightened as they begin to learn about the birth process and the importance of their own role in it. It is regrettable, however, that any father senses any element of coercion, no matter how subtle, and that any father is frightened away from a valuable learning experience. Just as it is important to find the right health care provider to attend your child's birth, it is important that you find a class and an instructor who can fill your needs in a nonpressured atmosphere. You might have to contact several instructors in your area before finding one with whom you and your partner are simpatico and whose curriculum stresses your interests.

How do you find classes in your community? Whom do you call? What kind of approach do you look for? How much do classes cost? How long is the series? What is covered in the individual classes? If you and your partner attend classes does it mean she must have a "natural" or "prepared birth" (without any medication)? It is useful to look at each of these questions in turn.

The best way to locate a childbirth class may be to ask your obstetrician or midwife for a recommendation. Often these health care providers recommend childbirth educators whose approach complements their own philosophy of childbirth. This is an important factor as it decreases the chance of any conflict between what the teacher says and what the doctor will do. Some physicians, however, are not familiar with local childbirth educators, and you may have to turn to your telephone directory to locate the classes offered in your community. Look under the general heading of "Social Services" or under the name of the particular organization. Among the most popular organizations are the American Society for Psychoprophylaxis in Obstetrics (ASPO), the original organization dedicated to teaching the Lamaze method of childbirth in the United States, International Childbirth Education Association, and the American Academy of Husband-Coached Childbirth. All these organizations are devoted to working with couples in preparation for childbirth and parenthood. Some new additions to this network are those groups that specialize in working with parents who expect a cesarean birth. Don't forget to check with your local hospital or Red Cross chapter. Both may offer classes in childbirth preparation.

Once you have identified some of these local groups, call them and find out where and when the classes are given. Most instructors conduct a series of six or eight classes and teach throughout the calendar year. The classes are held once each week and last approximately two hours. The entire series may cost between $15 and $90, depending on many factors. Some groups offer an introductory class and free film night to acquaint prospective parents with the philosophy of their organization. Take advantage of these free introductory classes; they provide you with a good opportunity to meet local instructors.

Some expectant fathers question the value of attending a full series of eight classes. After all, they reason, their wife won't be in the hospital more than two or three days. Why must they be in class for six to eight weeks? What can they expect to learn in these classes?

The classes cover a multitude of topics related to pregnancy and parenthood. Each class consists of a lecture, a demonstration, a question and answer period, a film, and refreshments. The early classes deal with the anatomy and physiology of pregnancy. Later classes deal specifically with techniques of childbirth preparation. Throughout the classes, there is open discussion of birth procedures—the routine and the controversial.

Sometimes, one of the most beneficial aspects of the classes is the sense of fellowship that develops among the pregnant couples. One father said, "I didn't believe that other men felt the way I did. It really felt good to hear another pregnant father say he was scared and was sure he wouldn't do the right thing at the right time." Another father remarked, "I was sure a lot of my wife's complaints were just to get my attention, but after I saw some of the other mothers and heard their stories of backaches, bellyaches, and leg cramps I began to understand that pregnancy really does take a lot out of a woman." Many couples develop lifelong friendships through these classes. It is rare to have the opportunity to meet couples in the same period of life, often with similar tastes, perhaps going to the same doctor and living in the same neighborhood. After your children are born it will be natural for you to visit one another. As your children grow, you may even send them to the same playgroup.

It is not our purpose here to include the entire content of childbirth classes. We will however, cover a sampling of some of the material available, both to give you some idea of the broad range of topics addressed and to introduce some terms and processes that are discussed more fully in subsequent chapters.

ANATOMY AND PHYSIOLOGY

Effacement and Dilation

The portion of the anatomy one is most concerned with during childbirth is the cervix, or mouth of the uterus. Normally the cervix is long, thick, and closed. During labor and delivery it opens (dilates) and thins out (effaces) to enable the baby to pass through to the vaginal canal and out into the world. Contractions of increasing intensity efface and dilate the cervix. Effacement is measured in terms of percentages. Ten percent effacement is common in early labor; at the time of delivery the cervix is 100 percent effaced. Dilation is measured in centimeters. At the beginning of labor the cervix may be dilated one or two centimeters; it needs to be dilated ten centimeters (almost four inches) for the baby to pass through.

A nurse, doctor, or midwife can measure degree of effacement and dilation by means of a sterile vaginal examination. Neither the intensity nor pain of contractions accurately indicates progress in labor.

Pelvic Measurements

The pelvis is a bony "girdle" that protects and houses the expanding and developing fetus. The critical concern is whether the baby's head will fit through the pelvis during delivery. The doctor or midwife can usually establish this by means of a vaginal examination. If it seems like a tight fit, the health care provider may suggest pelvimetry, an x-ray of the pelvic bones, to establish the available diameter through which the baby must pass.

Position of the Baby in the Pelvis

If the baby is in a "head first" position for delivery, this is called a vertex position. Breech position indicates that the baby's buttocks or feet are coming first. It is unlikely that a baby in vertex position will turn into a breech at the last minute.

However, even if the baby has settled into the pelvis with its head down, it can still rotate in a circular axis throughout labor and delivery. Usually at the time of birth, the back of the baby's head will face the front of the mother's pelvis. This is the ideal birth position, since in this position the baby's head fits best through the mother's pelvis.

Sometimes the back of the baby's head will face the mother's back. This is known as posterior position and usually means that the mother will experience what is known as "back labor," where the contractions are felt mostly in the lower back. To alleviate the discomfort of back labor, the laboring mother should be encouraged to turn from side to side or rest on her hands and knees. Firm counterpressure against the lower back also helps lessen back pain.

TESTS OF FETAL WELL-BEING

Sonogram

A sonogram is a picture made through the use of sound waves that indicates the location of the placenta, the size of the baby, and the number of babies in the uterus. Often it is used to confirm the gestational age of a baby so that mother and doctor can approximate the due date. Sonograms are not x-rays and do not produce radiation. As with any intervention, however, they should be administered only when necessary and for short periods of time.

Amniocentesis

In this procedure the doctor takes a sampling of amniotic fluid from the uterus through a needle stuck through the abdominal wall. When this test is done early in pregnancy, the doctor can determine whether certain chromosome defects exist, like the one which leads to mongolism. The baby's gender can also be determined from this test. When the test is done later in pregnancy, the information gained helps to establish whether or not the baby's lungs are mature. An amniocentesis may be done prior to an elective cesarean section to establish lung maturity of the unborn. The test may also be indicated if there is a history of Rh incompatability. Approximately one percent of mothers and infants who undergo amniocentesis experience problems directly related to the test. In other words it is a fairly safe procedure, but like other types of obstetrical intervention, it should be used only when indicated.

Nonstress Test

This test is usually performed when the pregnancy extends significantly past the due date. In this test the mother is placed on the fetal monitor, either at the hospital or at her doctor's office. The monitor depicts graphically how the baby's heartrate responds to the baby's own movement. A baby's heartbeat should increase slightly when the baby kicks *in utero*.

Estriol Blood Test

If the pregnancy has gone past due date, an estriol test may be done to establish the condition of the placenta. Estriol is a hormone secreted during pregnancy that assures the full functioning of the placenta. The placenta is designed to function for about forty weeks and may begin to deteriorate if the pregnancy goes past term. At the end of pregnancy a simple blood test done once a week (or more frequently) can establish that the placenta is still healthy and fully functional.

Stress Test

If the estriol blood test shows questionable results or, again, if the pregnancy has continued significantly past the due date, a stress test may be indicated. This test is performed at the hospital. The mother is placed on the fetal monitor just as in the nonstress test. However, in this procedure a medication called Pitocin, a synthetic uterine stimulant, is given intravenously. The dosage is adjusted carefully so that the woman begins to have contractions. When she has had a minimum of three contractions in ten minutes, the doctor watches to see how the fetal heart rate responds to these contractions. If the heartbeat pattern shows that the placenta is not functioning at full efficiency, delivery may be induced or a cesarean delivery may be performed. If the stress test indicates that the placenta is functioning well, the woman is sent home to await the natural onset of labor. Stress tests can be repeated once a week, or more frequently if needed.

CHILDBIRTH PREPARATION

Physical Conditioning

The many different methods of prepared childbirth all have one thing in common: an emphasis on maintaining the mother's good physical health during pregnancy. Rough sports are discouraged, but mothers are encouraged to keep in shape with a set pattern of body conditioning exercises or exercise like swimming or walking that promotes total body fitness. There are a number of exercise programs designed to help the pregnant woman maximize muscle strength and flexibility in those areas important for pregnancy and delivery. Subject to doctor's approval, these exercises should be done throughout pregnancy.

Relaxation

Another concept fundamental to all childbirth preparation classes is the emphasis on relaxation as part of the labor and delivery experience. Unfortunately, in this culture relaxation is one skill we neglect to teach our children. From an early age they learn that leisure time is usually spent in competitive or energetic pursuits and is not restful and calm.

Childbirth preparation classes teach relaxation techniques to both the man and the woman. The father is taught how to recognize signs of tension in his partner and how to give cues to relax that tension. With practice and patience the woman can eventually learn to relax at will, even under stressful circumstances such as labor. This ability to relax in the face of stress proves to be a skill of lifelong benefit and is especially handy during the first postpartum weeks.

Breathing Techniques

Specialized breathing techniques are sometimes taught as a method the woman may use to help control the discomfort of labor and to help the couple share total participation in the delivery experience. The type of breathing taught depends on the philosophy of the childbirth classes one attends. Most classes teach a sequential form of breathing, starting with slow breathing at the beginning of labor and moving to more complicated and intense breathing patterns at the end of labor. In addition to these patterns of breathing, you and your partner may learn special breathing techniques that help the mother push the baby out during delivery. It is vitally important that you learn the breathing techniques if you plan to "coach" your partner. The mother-to-be may become fretful or distracted during the latter stages of labor, and it will be up to you to help her get her breathing back on track.

These breathing techniques are neither magical nor mystical. They do not take away the pain generated by the contractions. However, they do give the woman in labor a tool she can use to cope with the contractions in a positive, self-controlled manner. They help a couple experience the birth of their baby in a wakeful, alert, participatory fashion.

HOSPITAL PROCEDURES

For many people the hospital carries a negative connotation; it is a place for sick people. Childbirth, however, is a happy exception. Most women go to the hospital in a healthy state in order to deliver a healthy baby. Although hospital births are not for everyone, they are preferred by the majority of women delivering babies in the United States at this time.

As with any institution, hospitals have policies and procedures that may alienate the pregnant couple. Good communication with your doctor or midwife will eliminate most of the fears associated with procedures that may be unfamiliar and possibly upsetting. Most couples do not realize that many procedures can be completely eliminated just on the basis of a word from their health care provider. In your childbirth classes and in your prenatal visits to your doctor or midwife, you may want to discuss the following procedures.

Consent Forms

Most hospitals have a standard preadmission procedure whereby you can indicate your insurance coverage and sign any necessary consent forms long before the moment when you report to the hospital in active labor. This is a real convenience as you can imagine the difficulty of trying to communicate the information needed for your partner's admission while she is having strong contractions. The consent forms usually state that you will allow your physician to perform the delivery and that you will agree to have anesthesia if there is an emergency or a problem. Even though you sign a consent form, you retain the right to a full explanation of any and all procedures.

Prep

The prep, or shaving of the pubic hair, used to be a routine procedure done on all pregnant women immediately preceding delivery. More recently it's been found that prepping does nothing to promote the health of the mother or the baby and can sometimes cause discomfort as the pubic hair grows back in. Many health care providers now prefer a partial prep (shaving only the bottom half of the pubic hair), a mini prep (shaving the pubic hair just around the vaginal opening), or a micro-mini prep (clipping particularly long hairs around the area where suturing may have to be done). To the relief of many women, a growing number of doctors require no prepping at all.

Enema

A regular soapsuds enema or smaller "Fleets" enema is often given to the mother in labor. It is intended to clean out the bowel to give as much room as possible to the descending baby and to alleviate the mother's fears of soiling the bed while pushing the baby out. The enema also helps the contractions get stronger. Enemas are usually not given if labor is far along, if the bag of waters has broken, or if there are any bleeding problems. An enema is also deferred if the woman has had a recent bout of diarrhea.

Fetal Monitor

The fetal monitor is a relatively new obstetrical instrument that allows the doctors and nurses to constantly monitor the baby's heart rate and the mother's contractions. Before fetal monitors were invented, nurses listened to the fetal heartbeat with a special stethoscope and monitored the mother's contractions by lightly touching her abdomen. Although nurses are still trained in this type of monitoring, they are sometimes unable to check these important signs as often as they would like because of an emergency or a busy workload. Monitors provide a continuous assessment of the baby's status and also generate a graphic printout of the wavelike labor contractions, useful to couples using special breathing techniques. Monitors are controversial because some people think that fetal distress is diagnosed too quickly, without giving the fetus a chance to stabilize or without considering the possibility of a false reading. This is linked by some to the increasing rate of cesarean deliveries. On the other hand, advocates of fetal monitors say that fetal distress is recognized faster so that intervention can be started immediately. It is wise to talk with your health care provider about the pros and cons of the monitor.

The fetal monitor can be used externally or internally. No matter how it is attached, it causes no discomfort, and the woman can still move to a comfortable position during labor without the feeling of being strapped down.

Pitocin

Pitocin is a medication that induces uterine contractions. It is used in the prenatal period for stress tests (see page 70). It can also be used to induce labor or to augment a desultory labor. After delivery, it is used to help the uterus contract and become firm and to prevent excess bleeding.

When Pitocin is given prior to or during labor, a small amount of the medication is mixed into a bottle of intravenous fluid and slowly dripped into the mother's bloodstream by means of an intravenous needle. After delivery, Pitocin is administered by intramuscular injection or intravenously if a bottle of intravenous fluid is already in place.

Medication for Pain

Pain medication is usually not considered a hospital procedure but more an individual decision between the pregnant couple and their health care provider. Before the delivery you and your physician or midwife need to discuss the various medication options available to you. There are three basic categories of medication that may be offered to the woman if she needs it.

Intramuscular Medications. These can include tranquilizers or analgesics. They do not take away the pain of labor but "take the edge off" the pain. Usually analgesics are combined with tranquilizers because pain is reduced more easily on relaxed muscles. The side effects these medications may have on both mother and baby depend on how much medication is administered and how soon before birth it is given. The most common analgesic medication offered in labor is Demerol (Meperidine HCl). A wide selection of tranquilizing agents is available. These medications often make the woman drowsy, which means that the coach has the added responsibility of keeping his partner alert so she can stay on top of her contractions with controlled breathing.

Local Anesthetic Blocks. These are given by means of an injection of a Novocain-type substance in a specific area, such as the cervical nerves (paracervical block) or perineal nerves (pudendal block). This type of medication does not take away pain completely but does dull the sensations of pain. A paracervical block is used during labor while the cervix is still dilating; a pudendal block is given in the delivery room prior to delivery.

Regional Anesthetic Blocks. These are used to totally eliminate the pain of labor. All these methods are considered safe. Side effects on baby and mother depend on the timing of the medication and the amount involved. The most common block is the lumbar epidural, used when the woman is in active labor. Usually this is administered by means of a thin, polyethylene catheter placed in the epidural space of the woman's back so that continuous doses of a Novocain-type medication can be offered as the anesthetic agent begins to wear off (in about one hour). Often, along with pain relief, the woman experiences loss of motor function in the legs and hips. This means she cannot get out of bed and may have trouble rolling from side to side. Because all sensations are blocked, it may be difficult for her to push the baby through the birth canal, necessitating the use of forceps at the time of delivery.

The caudal block is like an epidural but is given in a slightly lower area of the back. With the saddle block the medication is placed in the woman's spinal canal right before delivery, usually on the delivery table. It is not used to relieve the pain of labor contractions, only to eliminate the discomfort that results from pushing the baby down the birth canal.

HOSPITAL POLICIES

Hospital Tours

Hospital maternity units generally encourage pregnant couples to visit the hospital before birth to become familiar with the surroundings and with admission routines. Hospital tours also help you answer such questions as: Which entrance do we use? Where do we park at three in the morning? Where is the registration desk? Where does the father change clothes for delivery? Will the mother have a private or semiprivate room on the postpartum floor? Can the father take a shower during the hospital stay? How far is the nursery from the postpartum rooms? Can the father stay all day or just during visiting hours?

For an easy, uneventful admission to the hospital, you should be completely familiar with where you are going, how you will get there, and what will happen when you arrive. Also take a trial ride to the hospital—or perhaps two rides, one during rush hour and one when the roads are clear. Learn which entrances you should use at different times of the day and night, where the emergency entrance is located, and where you can leave your car.

Put pillows and blankets or towels in the car for your partner, and make sure you always have a full tank of gas. Have an extra set of keys available and some loose change at hand. Each of you should have a bag of supplies—packed well in advance. Your partner should also have contingency plans worked out in case labor begins when you are unavailable. These plans might call for assistance from reliable neighbors, a taxi, or the rescue squad.

Since there is no telling how long you will be in the hospital, you might as well be comfortable. If you and your partner have attended childbirth classes, you will have a small assortment of useful items to put in your bag. In addition, we recommend the following items:

- A hospital admission form, filled out completely.
- Several rolls of nickels and dimes for phone calls and vending machines.
- Phone numbers of the people you plan to call.
- A sandwich (prepared not too far in advance!) plus fruit, cookies, and other food to hold you over in case you can't leave the maternity unit. (You may, however, find that you are too busy to eat these things.)
- A clean shirt and undershirt. You will be working very hard during labor and no doubt you will want to change into fresh clothes after the birth.
- Insurance papers, permission paper for your attendance at the birth, your labor chart, and your notes from childbirth classes, as needed.
- A pad and pencil for keeping a diary of labor activity.
- Camera, film, flashbulbs, tape recorder, and tapes. (Some hospitals have an In-Hospital Birthing Photographic Service. This service costs little more than if you do the recording yourself, but it is reliable and you won't end up experiencing the birth from behind the viewfinder of your camera. There is

a lot to say for recording the birth of a baby, but there is more to say for watching it directly.)

- Cards, backgammon, chess, checkers, newspapers, and magazines—in case you need to pass the time in early labor.

Birthing Rooms

More and more hospitals are establishing birthing rooms for those women who want to give birth in a homelike atmosphere but want the advantages of safety and technical support that a hospital provides. Birthing rooms are essentially labor rooms equipped for the three-part process of labor, birth, and recovery. All functions are carried out in this one room. The room is used only for low-risk deliveries, with the understanding that if problems arise the mother is moved from the birthing room to a standard delivery setting.

If you and your partner are interested in a birthing room, you need to discuss this with your health care provider well in advance of your due date.

Fathers in Cesarean Delivery Settings

Many hospitals are now allowing fathers to be present during a cesarean delivery. This represents a rather radical change in hospital policy, since surgical procedures have always been considered off limits for observers. Because of the special character of the birth experience and because hospitals are coming to recognize the need to keep the family unit together, this new policy is slowly overtaking former prohibitions. (See Appendix I.) The couple must gain permission for the father to attend the cesarean delivery well in advance.

Sibling Visitation

Again, in an effort to keep the family unit together during this important time, some hospitals now allow sisters and brothers of the new infant to visit the maternity unit. This helps them feel included and also quells any fears they might have about the new baby or about the mother's safety.

POSTPARTUM INFORMATION

When you and your partner are in the midst of pregnancy, it is hard to believe there will ever be a postpartum period. But you will find that the pregnancy will indeed seem short, compared to the many years of childraising ahead. Childbirth classes deal with many topics common to the postpartum period, including those discussed below.

Characteristics of the Newborn

First-time parents are usually surprised by the appearance and temperament of a newborn. Babies who are only minutes or days old do not look or act like alert, chubby babies in the glossy pages of mothering magazines. On the contrary, newborns are wrinkled but cute. Eventually, you will come to think your child is the cutest on earth. (That's all right—it's allowed!)

Maternal Comfort Measures

After delivery, a woman can feel as if she has really been through the mill. Sometimes every bone and muscle aches. Classes teach comfort measures designed to relieve some of these aches and pains. Practical suggestions, such as ice packs and sitz baths, can be of real benefit.

Feeding

Childbirth classes rarely advocate one particular method of feeding the baby. Usually, a number of approaches are presented so the mother and father can decide which is best for them. There will generally be some discussion of schedule versus demand feeding and bottle versus breastfeeding.

Infant Care

It is not necessary here to discuss all the little chores that go into taking care of a baby. Childbirth classes stress the important point that infants are people, with human needs that they cannot express in words. Babies are quick to develop personalities of their own, and parents need to be sensitive to the whims and wishes of their infants. Much of parenting is actually intuitive, tempered with a soupçon of skill in areas such as feeding, diapering, and bathing. The most important skill new parents can bring to infant care is that of relaxation. Babies quickly pick up the tension they sense in their parents and respond in kind.

This chapter has attempted to provide a brief description of the way in which childbirth education classes can help prepare a man and a woman for a positive, shared, growth experience throughout pregnancy, childbirth, and parenting. Today's expectant parents are fortunate in having a wide variety of programs from which to choose. Almost every couple can find a program that is tailored to its own needs. You and your partner might want to begin early in pregnancy investigating those programs that are available in your area.

CHAPTER SIX

Choosing to Coach During Labor and Birth

As late as the 1950s the great majority of U.S. women were totally uneducated about labor and childbirth. In most cases they neither prepared for childbirth nor were forewarned about what they might experience. Many women assumed that the birth process was too painful to experience without drugs. Women in the early stages of labor were brought to the hospital by their husbands, then taken to rooms filled with other frightened, laboring women. Nurses and physicians appeared to do examinations and administer medicine. Nobody—neither doctors, nurses, nor the pregnant women themselves—considered the possibility of having fathers present to offer emotional support. Childbirth was a lonely, confusing, frightening affair.

At about the same time that Dr. Lamaze was doing his pioneering work in France, the British physician, Grantly Dick-Read was developing his own strategies designed to help women cope with childbirth. In 1942 Dick-Read's book *Childbirth Without Fear* was published. In it Dick-Read described his belief that pain in childbirth is the result of fear and a negative approach to birth based on generations of "old wives' tales." Dick-Read proposed eliminating fear, and thus pain, through knowledge, physical fitness, and relaxation.[36] Elsewhere in the world, however, coping strategies to help women deal with the discomfort of labor were being developed, even as early as the 1920s. In Russia at that time, some psychiatrists had started to investigate the application of hypno-suggestion for pain relief in childbirth. When these techniques were combined with the theories on conditioning developed by the Russian scientist, Pavlov, a new approach to childbirth began to evolve. In the late 1940s these Russian techniques were observed by a French obstetrician, Fernand Lamaze. During the next decade the notion of unmedicated childbirth spread throughout Europe. In 1958 Dr. Lamaze wrote *Painless Childbirth*, a book that presented the psychoprophylactic method he had been teaching pregnant women for years in France.[37] He called for the women to learn to work with, rather than fight, the contractions of labor, using breathing and muscle relaxation techniques. Lamaze wrote that a woman learns how to give birth without pain in the same way she learns to swim, write, or read; it was a matter of practice and conditioning. The presence of another person to coach the laboring woman's responses was an integral part of this system.

Although unnoticed for years by most Americans, these tools were available when the interest in humanizing childbirth took hold. In 1959 Marjorie Karmel popularized the Lamaze method for Americans in her short book, *Thank You, Dr. Lamaze*, setting the stage for expectant fathers to participate actively in the births of their children.[38]

The ideal birth is, of course, a highly individual experience. In researching this book we interviewed forty-seven men to find out which issues they considered to be fundamental. Many of the men we interviewed needed no persuasion to take an active role throughout their partners' pregnancies, including being their coach through labor and delivery. Some of these men said they could not imagine themselves participating less than fully. Many more men, however, became involved at the request of their partners.

In relating the stories of five couples, this chapter illustrates how some men made their decisions and how they reacted to the subsequent demands and rewards they experienced. Regardless of how fathers arrived at their decision to participate, they shared many concerns. Like the men described in Chapter Four, they had specific worries and fears about how things would turn out, they questioned their ability to be effective in their roles as coaches, and they felt somewhat alien as they approached the world of hospitals, labor and childbirth. Each case history presented here is followed by a brief discussion of the issues raised by that couple's experience. It is hoped that you will find your own concerns and expectations reflected in their stories.

JACK AND ROSEMARY: SHARING THE EXPERIENCE

Jack, who is now the father of three, decided to participate actively in the birth of his first child because such a decision was a logical extension of the relationship he and his wife shared as reliable, supportive friends. Rosemary was sure she wanted Jack with her throughout the birth. At the recommendation of their obstetrician, they attended childbirth classes to prepare themselves. Jack reported that he "just went along with the program." Although he viewed his upcoming role as coach as a reasonable arrangement, he still felt extremely apprehensive.

> *I never verbalized any negative feelings to Rosemary, but inside I felt differently. I had doubts about myself. Would I faint? Would I vomit? How would I react to seeing Rosemary in pain? Would I be useful? I just couldn't envision what would go on. There were times when I daydreamed about getting out of this, but the important things that happened in our lives had always been joint ventures. I believe refusal would have had adverse effects on our relationship, and I think, for my part, I always would have regretted not being there.*

Before their classes started Jack and Rosemary attended a childbirth film. Jack reported that the film made him feel a little queasy. He hoped that he would feel differently when it was his own wife and child. As their Lamaze classes proceeded, Jack began to feel less helpless and more confident. Nonetheless, he did not completely understand what his role was to be. He was afraid that he might have to help Rosemary with her breathing during contractions, and he did not want to have that responsibility. Also he felt uncomfortable at the prospect of seeing Rosemary in what might be a difficult and "unladylike" situation. Finally, he was worried that his uncertainty about everything would affect his performance.

One Tuesday morning Jack received a call from Rosemary shortly after he had arrived at work. She told him that contractions had started, and while they were about fifteen minutes apart and not very intense, she felt scared and nervous. Jack headed for home. He arrived to find that the one-minute-long contractions had increased in intensity and were now coming every five or seven minutes. He called their obstetrician and was directed to take Rosemary to the hospital. It was now close to 11:00 A.M. Jack remembered feeling extremely relieved that he would not have to make this journey in rush-hour traffic.

Once he and Rosemary were both settled in the hospital labor room, Jack found himself "running after a very fast train." Reconsidering this remark, Jack said, "No. I felt I had been *hit* by a very fast train. I just wasn't prepared for the intensity of it." At the nurse's direction, he provided counterpressure to Rosemary's lower back. He also fed her ice chips, held her hand, and talked to her. He encouraged her through the contractions and communicated information he overheard from the staff.

Jack recalled that during most of her labor he received no feedback from Rosemary. She seemed so distant and he felt alienated from her. This aspect of the experience was disturbing, and he found himself wondering what she would be like when it was all over. He was convinced that his presence was of no help to her.

When Rosemary was instructed to start pushing, Jack's involvement grew and his feelings began to change. When a nurse indicated that they could see some of the baby's head, Jack became excited and joined the staff in cheering on Rosemary's pushing efforts. "I had pictured this birth as a really messy business," he remembered, "and thought I wouldn't mind labor as much as delivery. Actually, labor was harder. By the time birth was imminent, I was really hyped up and ready for my baby to be born." The doctor and Jack changed into scrub suits while the nurses wheeled Rosemary's labor bed into the delivery room. When Jack arrived in the delivery room, only minutes later, Rosemary was already on the delivery table and the nurses were adjusting the stirrups for her legs. Jack said he felt a little lightheaded. He sat down on a stool next to Rosemary and held her hand.

Jack felt a surge of emotion as the baby was born. "It's worth all that goes before," he said. "I've witnessed my three children being born. Each time I've experienced a unique high. Each time the intensity was the same. I'm honestly filled with awe. I don't believe any other experience could do that to me." Rosemary shared Jack's euphoria at the completion of each birth.

Jack's memories of the recovery room were vivid. As he and Rosemary gazed lovingly at their first daughter, he was amazed that she returned their glances. The baby seemed very interested in her new surroundings and spent some time nursing. While still in the recovery room, cradling their new baby in their arms, Jack and Rosemary called their relatives and a few friends. Jack remembers feeling physically drained but elated; everyone was so healthy!

Jack said he felt shell-shocked for a couple of weeks following the intensity of this experience; for an even longer time he experienced considerably reduced libido. During these weeks, he and Rosemary began talking about their reactions to the birth, and only then did he learn that he had provided specific and valuable assistance to her during labor and delivery. She was able to tell him in detail just how he had helped. Rosemary saw Jack's participation as crucial to her having had a positive experience. Jack believes their relationship is a closer one because they participated as a team in such a meaningful endeavor. They had done something difficult and demanding together.

When it came time for the births of their second and third children, there was more information available about the use of drugs in childbirth. Jack said that he and Rosemary had become more concerned about avoiding medication. Thus, Jack came to view his coaching role as even more necessary.

Jack was among the many men who told us they became involved in childbirth primarily at their partner's initiative. One father suggested how this happens. When a man is asked by a woman he loves to support her in childbirth, he may be hesitant about the idea. Yet he thinks to himself, "Maybe I should learn more about why this is important to her." He starts to read and think about the issues. He wonders what it's like to wait outside the labor and delivery rooms and not know what's going on. As he begins to learn about the positive ways that he can help, his qualms start to subside and his enthusiasm grows. He finds himself wanting to be present at the birth, and even more, to be a participant in it. Fathers begin to share their partner's convictions that being in control is better than being controlled. Although the whole experience still carries an element of fear with it, this fear is balanced by the excitement of the joint endeavor. In the end their willingness to participate is often a mixture of duty and excitement.

Although men like Jack are able to make the commitment to share the childbirth experience with their partners, they are not free from a host of concerns and worries. They are concerned about the safety and health of the mother and baby and are afraid of medical complications. They worry about their partner becoming uncommunicative, upset, or irritable. Many worry that they will have trouble remaining calm and supportive in a situation that they may find to be emotionally trying. One father compared his feelings to those of a platoon commander in combat. "In both situations," he remarked, "others are looking to you for guidance and reassurance at a time when you are just as nervous as they are."

Some men fear that they will not get to the hospital on time, or they may be afraid that once there, they will either be ignored or ordered around. Many men worry that they will feel nauseated or faint while participating in childbirth, but this almost never happens. One father reported that the prospect of seeing blood made him very leery, but when his wife's I.V. came out and blood began to drip down her arm, he calmly told the nurse. He was surprised by his own nonchalance. Expectant fathers also wonder if the breathing and relaxation techniques they learned and practiced in childbirth classes will be of use when their partner is experiencing real contractions. (The women wonder about this too!) Many men worry that they will not be able to tell when a contraction begins. Finally, perhaps ironically, many fathers-to-be are concerned that, after all their preparation, they will somehow miss their child's birth. One father said, "I'll be so damn mad if I'm at work and unable to get home or to the hospital on time. I'll feel like telling my wife, 'Wait! Don't go! You can't have the baby without me!'"

In the last two decades or so, birth in this country has come to be recognized as a natural, healthy process. The emphasis has begun to shift away from the mechanics of the process; more and more attention is being focused on the emotional well-being of the laboring woman. The presence of a reliable and supportive coach throughout labor and birth has both psychological and physiological benefits for the mother. Many women, like Rosemary, do not want to face the unfamiliar demands of childbirth without a close ally. In addition, when the birth takes place outside the familiar home environment, the impersonal and complex routines of a hospital setting can provoke fear and anxiety.[39] Such emotions have in fact been found to produce adverse biological effects in the woman, altering uterine motility and blood flow.[40] And these effects in turn result in a more tense and painful delivery. It is a fact that women who are attended by prepared coaches report less pain during labor and use less medication in delivery.[41] Furthermore, only those who have continual support report "raptures" and a "peak of experience" during birth.[42] In short, your participation as coach can be indispensable to your partner and to your child's healthy, joyful birth.

While many fathers reported that they felt useless or ineffectual during their partner's labor, most women replied that they were amazed that their coaches didn't realize the degree to which they were helpful and necessary. This kind of misunderstanding seems related to the inability of many women to divide their attention between the serious internal business of labor and their interactions with the outside world. One woman told us, "Advanced labor is just not the time for conversation. No one expects a weightlifter to chat in the middle of *his* job." For some men this lack of communication was, not surprisingly, one of the most difficult aspects of coaching.

Only after the birth can many women express their gratitude to their partners for their support in the birthing process. In the quiet time after birth, in the hours or days that follow, new mothers are able to reflect on their partners' contributions. In the words of some of the women we spoke to:

> *Bob was my saving grace. I felt so tired and frustrated for most of my labor. . . . His support and knowledge really kept me going.*

> *The staff was very encouraging. They were an emotional help, too, but John was my strength. I don't think I could have done it without him. He was so patient and understanding, and his faith in me played an important role in my labor.*

> *While I didn't talk to Bill much during my labor, I always knew he was near me. I heard everything he said to me or to the nurses or to the doctor. His voice was so important. It was my contact with something familiar and tender as I went through a labor that was unfamiliar and often harsh. I needed to hold his hand, too. I feel a tremendous sense of sadness when I think about a woman who must go through childbirth without a best friend with her.*

> *His presence seemed to make my labor and the birth of our child valid.*

> *I realize that I probably would have gotten through the whole thing without Ray, but I thank my lucky stars that I didn't have to. . . . Having the man you love with you is worth more than all the professionals in the world.*

BRIAN AND IVA: BIRTH AS AN AWE-INSPIRING EXPERIENCE

To Brian, participating in the births of his two children was the normal thing to do. He said later he couldn't imagine himself not having been there. Together he and Iva planned how they wanted each of the two births managed. Because Brian said he always needs to know as much as possible about anything that affects their lives, he read about childbirth, talked to other people about their experiences, and went to see the obstetrician with Iva early in her pregnancy. As he and Iva evaluated what was known about factors that affected the newborn, they became increasingly committed to a nonmedicated labor and birth. For this, Lamaze preparation seemed essential to them. Brian said that he enjoyed the classes, which began at a time when he and Iva were beginning to feel the pregnancy would never end. He found that practicing relaxation and breathing at home was an emotional release because it made him feel the birth was imminent.

Brian talked to us about the births of his two children, Stacy, who was four, and Kristin, who was one. For him the two experiences were very different. The first labor was long and tiring, exactly what he and Iva expected. Yet, overall, he felt that they had been able to stay with the contractions and maintain control. Brian remembered feeling annoyed at the nurses who repeatedly offered Iva drugs "to take the edge off," even though he and Iva had clearly stated their wish not to use medication. Brian was sure that Iva would know when and if she needed something.

When Iva's contractions slowed to thirty-minute intervals, the doctor gave her Pitocin. Instantly, the contractions quickened, coming one on top of the other. Brian found that he helped Iva most by timing each contraction aloud so that she knew when the peak of intensity was over and could anticipate the relaxation she would experience in the brief lull before the next contraction began.

Brian remembered feeling relief and amazement as Stacy was born—relief that she was whole and healthy and that Iva's discomfort was over, and amazement that he and Iva suddenly had another person in their family. He was also amazed by the mechanics of the birth process. He was struck by the speed with which the rest of Stacy's body slipped out once her head emerged, and how quickly her color changed from blue to pink. Afterward, Brian was emotionally and physically exhausted. He felt ravenously hungry and ready to go home to sleep within an hour of the birth.

Brian said that although he and Iva had had to force themselves to go to childbirth classes for the second child, they were pleased that they had gone. They learned a lot more from the classes the second time around and felt better prepared for this birth than they had for their first. Brian felt much less the "scientific observer" and had what he described as a somewhat mystical experience. When Iva's membranes ruptured, Brian became lightheaded and took time to get something to eat. Suddenly he found himself very relaxed, and his mind seemed exceptionally clear. During this period he had some valuable and revealing insights about himself and about Iva. He felt elated; he was on an emotional and intellectual high.

Kristin's birth was much easier and less exhausting. Labor lasted only four hours, and Kristin was born after only four pushes. This time nobody offered Iva medication. In fact, at one point when Iva was having trouble and she and

Brian were struggling to reestablish her breathing pattern, the doctor stepped out so they could work together in private. Brian appreciated that gesture tremendously.

After Kristin's birth, Brian and Iva both felt euphoric. Brian wanted to see and hold Kristin right away. But she had to be taken to the nursery until her body temperature had stablized. Brian recalled feeling wonderful as he waited with Iva until the baby was brought back to them. He called home to tell Stacy the news. When Kristin was finally brought into Iva's room, Brian held her snugly and cooed at her. He remembers that she opened her eyes briefly before nodding off to sleep.

Brian reported that from the time he and Iva first contemplated having children, he always imagined himself being present at the births. This self-generated interest contrasts with the experience of other men whose interest in participating in childbirth was initially, and sometimes solely, motivated by their partners' desire that they be there.

Men who share Brian's motivation see the chance to witness childbirth as a rare and priceless opportunity to experience the mystery of birth. As one father described it, the concept of "regeneration" seemed to be an essential part of the magnetism of birth. "Birth is the closest thing to a supernatural event in normal life. Sharing the event becomes at times a secular religion, and descriptions of the joys of childbirth suggest a transcendent experience."[43] The mystical aspect of birth has been with mankind for eons. Both ancient and modern religions include accounts of mystical supernatural births—Athena springing from the head of Zeus, Jesus born of a virgin mother. Some fathers seem uncomfortable with this aspect of birth. "It's difficult and embarrassing for most adult professional people to admit that childbirth is still basically a mystery, a piece of magic, a mystical experience, and an altered state of consciousness."[44] Other fathers like Brian accept the mystery, revel in it, and benefit and grow from it.

For Brian there was a natural curiousity about how the process of birth takes place. Most of us can share his amazement at the engineering of the human body. Who has not wondered how such a big baby can emerge from such a small opening? Many men who attended childbirth classes also reported how fascinated they were by the diagrams portraying the physical changes the woman undergoes during pregnancy. One father said, "It is unbelievable that a uterus that is normally two inches long can stretch to accommodate a six-pound baby, let alone a bigger one!" Another pointed out how incredible it was that the mother's other organs still functioned relatively smoothly when they had been totally displaced by the bulk of a baby. One father was struck by the faithfulness with which the woman's body goes through the individual stages of labor and birth. Another was astonished that a baby only one minute old could nurse without reading books on how to do it!

Fathers who had always pictured themselves at the births of their children frequently mentioned another reason why attending was important to them. Many viewed the event as more than the birth of their child; it was the birth of their family. One asked, "How could I miss such an important event?" Several men mentioned looking forward to the day when they could tell their children that they had been at their births. These fathers expected that it would be important for their children to know how much they cared.

Iva's and Brian's desire to avoid medication is a common one, based on an informed picture of the hazards of drugs. There is increasing awareness that drugs taken by a pregnant woman can have potentially toxic effects on the developing fetus. The warning issued by the Committee on Drugs of the American Academy of Pediatrics states, "There is no drug which has been proven safe for the unborn child."[45] Drugs used during labor and birth have been shown to affect newborns by producing drowsiness, irritability, and jitteriness in the first days of life.[46] A significantly higher percentage of infants of medicated than unmedicated mothers suffer oxygen deprivation and heartrate deceleration.[47,48] Some drug effects go unrecognized for long periods of time, only to become manifest after many years.

In addition to the very negative effects drugs can have on the newborn, another reason to avoid using drugs during labor and childbirth is that their use increases the likelihood that other interventions will be necessary. Even the epidural—which appears to be the safest anesthetic, with minimum effect on the baby—is capable of slowing labor down, making induction (via a second drug) necessary. Because an epidural impairs a woman's sensations, forceps and episiotomies tend to become routine when epidurals are administered.[49]

We do not mean to imply that drugs should never be used. But whenever possible, a couple should try to proceed without medication.

BOB AND JUDY: A DIFFICULT ORDEAL

Bob and Judy had their first three children in the "traditional" fashion. Each time, Judy had been alone and medicated for labor and childbirth. When she became pregnant a fourth time, Judy said she wanted to try Lamaze preparation. Bob recalled that he did not have a strong opinion one way or the other. He agreed to attend the birth because Judy wanted him to.

By the time he and Judy had completed the childbirth classes, Bob was feeling that his participation was "probably a good thing." He reported that he did not have any real worries since "Judy had successfully given birth to children three times before and she did it without me. I just figured she would have another baby. . . only this time I'd be there."

Judy's labor began on a Sunday evening. She had just finished bathing their two youngest children, and Bob was reading a bedtime story to all of them. Judy interrupted storytime to tell Bob that mild contractions had begun and had been regular for the last hour.

Judy changed her clothes and then made a sandwich for Bob. He called his sister who would stay with the children. He also called the obstetrician. Since this was Judy's fourth pregnancy and since she was already past her due date, the doctor told them to head for the hospital. Judy hugged and kissed each child, and Bob reminded them that they would come to the hospital in a day or two to visit their mom and see their new baby.

Bob and Judy drove to the hospital. Before being officially admitted, Judy was checked by a nurse. Bob was disappointed to hear that she was only two centimeters dilated and that contractions had slowed down. The nurse checked with Judy's doctor by phone and then directed Judy and Bob to return home and wait for the labor to progress further.

Later Bob recalled that he had felt embarrassed that they had gone to the hospital before it was time. He knew Judy was disappointed, too, so he suggested that they not return home right away. Instead, they went to a Chinese restaurant where Judy had tea in the midst of occasional contractions, and Bob had a full meal.

They arrived home at 11 P.M. and went to bed. By 3 A.M. they were on their way to the hospital once again. Judy was clearly in active labor at this point. Checking in to the hospital was quick and easy. Bob remembered feeling pleased that he had mailed in their completed registration forms a few weeks earlier. A nurse brought a wheelchair to take Judy to Labor and Delivery. Bob waited at the front desk to sign the remaining forms. When he got upstairs to Labor and Delivery, he saw a sign on the double doors that said "Restricted Area. No Admittance."

"Then my stomach got tight," he recalled. "I wondered if I was in the right place. Then I wondered if I should really be there at all." He remembers taking a deep breath and striding through the doors. A nurse met him and led him to the labor room where he was reunited with Judy. She seemed so relieved to see him, even though they had been separated only twenty minutes.

Judy's labor was long and more difficult than Bob had expected. He remembered being very tense because Judy seemed to be in so much pain. He relied heavily on the nurses for direction and reported that they were very active and supportive during Judy's labor. Bob spent his time feeding Judy ice chips, wiping her brow with a cool cloth, and talking to her in a soothing and encouraging way. At 6:40 A.M. when her cervix was about six centimeters dilated, Judy's contractions were coming very hard and fast. She said she could not continue without medication. She was losing control and Bob was unable to get her to concentrate on her breathing. When the nurse told her she could make it, she became very upset. The doctor eventually concurred with Judy and ordered an epidural because she was so tired and her muscles were so tense. Although Bob would have preferred an unmedicated labor, as they and the obstetrician had discussed earlier, he heard the doctor's judgment with relief. "I didn't want her to have the pain. It seemed wrong to force her to 'live up to' a goal set before she knew how long and hard labor would be." Once the drugs took hold, Judy relaxed.

When Judy was fully dilated she was moved to the delivery room. The bright lights, shiny equipment, and cold temperature made Bob feel uncomfortable. He remembered thinking that he did not belong in this "operating room," especially after their "secure and familiar labor room." After several minutes of pushing, their baby was born. Bob stayed at Judy's side for a few minutes, then walked out of the delivery room. "It had just been too much," he remarked, "It had taken so long. I needed a break from the whole thing."

Bob joined Judy and the baby in the recovery room. Although he had heard that fathers who witness birth feel an immediate attachment to their new baby he did not experience that. "I was more concerned with Judy," he said. "We were so glad it was over. And I wanted to get a vasectomy. It wasn't until I called the other children—they were so excited—that I started to relax and really think about the baby and our family."

As Bob looked back on this experience in childbirth, he could not say he liked it. He saw himself as having been a rather average coach and remarked that his and Judy's relationship did not lend itself comfortably to a "coach-coachee" arrangement. Actually he had envisioned himself playing a greater role than he actually felt he had taken. "It was tough," he said later. "For me it wasn't the wonderful, mystical experience you hear some men talk about. . . . I don't know if we would have had all the other children had I seen the first one born. You appreciate what women do so much more after being there." In spite of the fact that Bob felt uncomfortable during much of the labor and delivery, he believed it was a valuable and worthwhile experience. He claimed, with some satisfaction, "At least I was with her."

His effort and willingness were not lost on Judy, who described her other birth experiences as "lonely." She remarked, "I think he did it just for me. I could tell parts of it upset him. But it really enhanced our relationship; it made us just a little more intimate. It's such a personal thing, and we went through it together. I give him a lot of credit. After all, I realize *I* didn't have a choice; I *had* to be there. Bob had a choice."

Although Bob's reaction was among the most ambivalent we heard, many fathers who were interviewed did not experience a feeling of elation from participating in childbirth. Many reported they did not like labor. "It's not something I'd choose to do on a Saturday night," said one. Another father explained that while his wife viewed their joint participation in the birth of their first child as romantic, he found it to be a long, tedious, frustrating, and frightening experience. When this father's second child came so quickly that he missed the birth, he reported no regrets. Instead, he said he felt relieved that everything had happended so easily and that everyone was in good health.

A number of fathers shared Bob's immediate reaction of "never again." Most reported relief that "the ordeal" was over, and that mother and baby were healthy. For some men, the relief was fleeting; for others it constituted an overwhelming emotion. A few fathers said it was the first time since the beginning of the pregnancy that they could totally relax. One man told us he cried after his son was born, as much out of emotional release as from seeing the new baby. Certainly the length and difficulty of labor are important factors in the intensity of these reactions.

Several men reiterated that the work of labor and childbirth can be tense and demanding for the father who participates. "The inevitability of the process can be frightening," remarked one father. Nonetheless, most men maintained that nothing matched the overwhelming sensations of the birth itself and the sense of completion and satisfaction that follow.

DAVID AND CAROLYN: USING THE BIRTHING ROOM

David and Carolyn, pregnant with their first child, enjoyed attending a series of prepared childbirth classes. David was somewhat surprised at how involved he became in the classes since he hadn't looked forward to two hours of "instruction" after working a full day. He said that most of their friends had also attended classes and had been positive in their reports of childbirth. "Actually," David remarked, "I think the dads rave about the whole experience of childbirth more than the mothers do."

As a result of information they received in class, David and Carolyn decided to use the new birthing room they had seen on a tour of their hospital. The room had a warm, homey atmosphere. Its large bed, comfortable chairs, wallpaper and curtains provided a stark contrast to the impersonal chrome-and-tile atmosphere of the regular labor and delivery rooms. "The delivery room gave me the impression of 'emergency' or 'complications,'" he said. "It just looked too serious. I figured that if everything went all right for us, Carolyn could just deliver our baby on the comfortable bed in the birthing room. It presented a calmer picture to me." David realized, too, that if complications arose, the delivery room and its specialized medical and surgical equipment were close at hand.

In discussing his motivations for participating in childbirth, David explained that he had been strongly encouraged by the positive reactions of other men. He said he knew that his presence would be good for his wife, but initially he saw it as important for himself. "It means more than having a cigar and a drink," he said. "The way I see it, my wife is not the only beneficiary." David also believed that his willing participation in this shared experience would make a difference in their relationship. He saw it as a way they would learn more about each other and remarked, "I expected Carolyn would see me differently after this."

Carolyn's labor started easily on a Sunday morning. They both felt relaxed and ready for birth. Within an hour, David realized that labor was moving along faster than they had anticipated. Carolyn was experiencing lower back pain that could be relieved only when David pushed firmly against her back with the heel of his hand. He remembered that their last hour at home was "a circus." Carolyn found it most comfortable to sit on the floor. During contractions he pushed against her back. In between contractions he had only two or three minutes to help her put on each piece of clothing. Finally, they were in the car. Carolyn rode in the back seat.

Once in the birthing room, Carolyn changed into a hospital gown. David was instructed to change into a blue scrub suit. He later remarked,

> *I really felt official, dressed in that hospital stuff. I remember thinking how odd it was that everyone acted as though I dressed like this all the time. The truth was I was so impressed with this routine. I asked Carolyn how I looked. She just smiled. I was really enjoying what was going on. I was nervous enough to be excited, but I wasn't really scared.*

Carolyn's labor continued to progress quickly. Within an hour of being admitted, she was beginning the most difficult phase of labor, known as transition. David said that at this point he was very grateful for having attended their childbirth classes, for Carolyn's transition was intense and she responded as he had learned she might.

> *She acted as if she were angry at me. She didn't say anything, but she gave me dirty looks. I got one of those looks everytime I told her to relax, or told her she was doing a good job or that the contraction was almost over. I had been giving her massages earlier and this had seemed to soothe her. Now she pushed my hand aside and clearly didn't want me to touch her. I remembered our Lamaze teacher telling us that irritability was common during transition. She had cautioned us not to take anything personally. Still, I felt a little uncomfortable, especially when I knew the nurse could see what was going on.*

David reported that once Carolyn was fully dilated and was allowed to push, the whole atmosphere changed. There was much excitement in the birthing room. Carolyn's pushing was very effective, and in less than an hour, she was ready to deliver. She and David held hands. At the doctor's instruction, Carolyn gave a strong, slow push and their baby's head was delivered. David said he had a momentary panicky feeling because the sound of the doctor suctioning the mucous out of the baby's mouth and nose made him uneasy. The baby uttered a single cry, and then Carolyn gave another push. Their son was born. David and Carolyn were crying and laughing and hugging out of relief and joy."I felt drunk!" David recalled.

Once the umbilical cord had been cut, the nurse handed the baby to David while Carolyn delivered the placenta. David gently rocked his son in his arms. He remembered speaking to him a little, but "mostly I just kept looking at him, and I touched his hands." Once Carolyn moved into a comfortable position on the bed, David placed their child in her arms; she offered the baby her breast and he began to nurse. David took pictures of Carolyn and their son, and then the doctor took the first pictures of the new family.

Many of David's remarks reflect an attitude expressed by several men we interviewed. They saw themselves *primarily* as one of the main characters in the drama of pregnancy and childbirth. That is, while they recognize their ability to coach and support their partners and regard this as essential, they view many aspects of the childbirth experience as personal and critical to their own development. They do not measure their involvement only in terms of its benefit to their partners, but often think of their participation as useful or necessary or pleasurable for themselves.

Some recent research conducted among expectant fathers who attended Lamaze classes indicates similar findings.

> *These expectant fathers do not conceptualize themselves as mainly supportive figures. They had a sense that, like their wives, they too were experiencing an important development in their lives. So often, the expectant father is seen as being secondary. Although his actions, whether they be helping in the delivery room or assisting through difficult times during the pregnancy, may be viewed by his wife, friends, family, health care professionals, as supportive, the expectant father views these activities as central to his experience as an expectant father.*[50]

David's belief that Carolyn would see him differently after the birth of their child reflects his recognition that he *would* be different. He would be a father now, a man who had attended the birth of his child. Although he was not sure about the implications of all this, he sensed that the difference would be a positive one. He had begun to consider his new relationships—the one with his wife, the other with his child.

It seems natural that fathers-to-be would contemplate how their lives might be different after the birth. These concerns cannot be resolved ahead of time, but they are worth considering and discussing during pregnancy. Some couples find that a number of their concerns are reduced as a result of childbirth classes.

David and Carolyn attended Lamaze classes with six other couples in the home of a trained instructor. In this relaxed atmosphere they felt free to ask questions and discuss their concerns. At the end of the series, most men reported that they felt prepared for labor and delivery. Said one participant, "Our instructor told us the good, the bad, and the ugly. I felt I had heard the whole story and wouldn't be too surprised or caught offguard." David later remarked that this preparation was invaluable in helping him cope with the rejection he felt during the transition phase of Carolyn's labor.

The overwhelming sense of awe and attachment David felt as he held his son for the first time has been called engrossment.[51] This term refers to the feelings of absorption a father can feel if he is allowed to spend some time with his new baby. The newborn can have a significant impact on the father; the father becomes preoccupied with his offspring and with what this new person could mean to him. It is significant that David remembered touching his son's hands, for it seems that visual cues do not satisfy the father's needs. Physical contact is one of the most meaningful ways to communicate and appears to be crucial in establishing a strong bond between father and child.[52] (You may want to refer back to Chapter Four for more discussion of parent-child bonding.)

GORDON AND JONI: HOME BIRTH

Gordon and Joni had their first baby at home. This was the second marriage for each of them, and they had deliberated seriously whether or not to have a baby. They shared the feeling that birth was a very important, private, family affair, and they felt strongly they wanted to keep their baby with them all the time. "In a hospital," Gordon said, "you never know if you will have to make a fuss to keep the baby, and I am just not that type."

In her training as a physician, Joni had seen many unpleasant occurrences in hospital obstetric units. She felt that too often the staff had little regard for the psychological well-being of mother, father, or baby. Hospital births seemed dehumanizing to her. Thus, long before she became pregnant, she began reading about home birth experiences and discussing this possibility with Gordon. The idea was not new to him because two of his three siblings had been born at home in Nebraska. Despite this previous positive exposure, he commented that he would not have considered having their baby at home if Joni had not been a doctor. In his words, "At least I had the fantasy that she would know what to do if something went wrong."

When Joni became pregnant, they carefully explored whether the home birth options available to them were safe enough to consider seriously. Their first concern was for the safety of their child. In a nearby suburb, they found a maternity center that offered the services of three licensed nurse-midwives who helped plan home births. In addition to attending at the delivery, the nurse-midwife provided comprehensive care for pregnant and newly delivered couples.

Gordon and Joni were so impressed by the quality of care, they decided to go ahead with their plans to have their baby at home. They also chose and visited a backup hospital in case difficulties occurred. They enrolled in the center's Lamaze classes. Gordon reported that they received scant encouragement from their friends and relatives, including Joni's colleagues—this in spite of the fact that their home birth arrangement was probably among the best available in the country.

Joni's labor began five days before her due date, as she and Gordon were watching the basketball playoffs on television. Joni hadn't eaten dinner because she was "feeling funny." Gordon had a sense of what was happening and remembered remarking to her, "If we're going to have the baby tonight, do you think you could wait until the end of the game?" They were in bed, watching television, and as the evening wore on, Joni dozed on and off. Then with four minutes remaining in the game, she turned to Gordon and said, "I know the game isn't over yet, but could you time my contractions now? I have to concentrate on breathing."

Gordon remembered feeling surprised. Joni hadn't told him that her contractions had begun. He said that he felt really "up." He had just watched a great game, his team had won, and he was excited and ready for their baby to be born.

After they had timed Joni's contractions for an hour, Gordon called the nurse-midwife. The birth attendant arrived at 2 A.M., and the midwife arrived soon after. Gordon was amused when he heard the nurse-midwife ask the birth attendant to boil water. His mind raced to the scenes in old movies where boiling water played an important part of every home medical procedure. He could only laugh when the birth attendant later appeared with a cup of tea for each of them.

Gordon and the birth attendant had already stripped the bed and remade it with a clean sheet on the bottom, topped by a shower curtain and another clean sheet. Joni chose to labor sitting on the edge of the bed. Gordon got a kitchen stool and sat in front of her. Between contractions, she rested against him.

Joni's labor was long and hard. There was back labor that was difficult to relieve. During one lull, Gordon, Joni, and the midwife all stretched out next to each other on the bed. "We were so relaxed," he exclaimed. "Such a moment could never have been possible in a hospital."

Gordon reported that, difficult as it was, they felt they had never cooperated as fully or had done anything as meaningful together in their lives. He remembered being continually impressed throughout the labor with the nature of the process. They were both working hard physically, harder than ever before; at the same time, labor was progressing as if by natural forces beyond their control. It was as if the baby was being born according to some preestablished plan. Gordon felt totally exhausted; he also felt exhilarated. He was completely involved, and Joni needed him very much. Through a look in her eyes, or an embrace, she let him know she was relying on him to help her maintain control. Gordon felt proud of her for working so hard and doing so well. At one point he remembered feeling a kind of anger toward the baby because Joni was making such an effort and nothing seemed to be happening. Gordon said his main apprehension throughout the labor was that something would happen that would persuade their midwife that they should go to the hospital. He was afraid Joni's labor would stop progressing or the fetal heartrate would drop.

After thirteen hours of labor, Joni had to push for two hours. When the baby was finally born, Gordon felt relieved, proud, and thankful that everything had turned out fine and that they were all together at home.

The birth attendant cleaned up the room and took the soiled sheet and shower curtain off the bed. The midwife prepared lunch for everyone, and then, after eleven hours in attendance, both left. Gordon remembered feeling such peace and fulfillment as he and Joni fell asleep in their own bed with their son between them.

If, like Joni and Gordon, you are considering having your baby at home, you are taking on added responsibilities. Thus, it is especially important that you examine all the factors involved.

Home birth has many things to recommend it, apart from the warmth and support. The father is able to participate freely, uninhibited by rules; other children may take part; and the mother can follow her own body rhythms without interference. There is no mother-baby separation and baby-parent bonding can occur without interruption. But home birth is not for everyone. Even in countries such as Holland and Britain where home birth is made a safe alternative by "flying squads" and superbly trained midwives, many women birth in hospitals—and complications can occur no matter how healthy and well-prepared the woman.[53]

Many people are uncomfortable with the idea of having their babies at home. Sometimes, even with the closest couples, the partners differ in their attitudes toward home birth. One midwife who shared her experiences with us[54] emphasized the importance of communication between expectant partners who are considering home birth. She has observed that the two partners are likely to differ with respect to such issues as their desire to avoid hospitals and the degree of participation envisioned for each. Interestingly, prospective fathers often feel more strongly about having their babies at home than do their partners. No matter who is the stronger advocate, a couple must resolve their differences before the birth occurs. If either partner feels coerced, it will undermine the joyfulness of the experience. For Gordon and Joni, the intense feelings of exhilaration and involvement were a natural result of the cooperation and understanding that had evolved between them as they worked through their plans for the birth. Together they had explored and evaluated their home birth options and their backup plans in case a hospital became necessary.

Home births are on the upswing in the United States. Some feel that the real challenge introduced by the home birth movement is to humanize and simplify childbirth management in hospitals. Some hospitals are now experimenting with birthing rooms or maternity centers as alternatives to traditional care. The low-risk woman has the advantage of not having to rush to a cold, unfamiliar delivery room at the most uncomfortable time of labor. For the couple who eschews a hospital birth but is not comfortable with the risks of a home delivery, the birthing room or maternity center is likely to be ideal.

Some of the fathers we spoke to mentioned their satisfaction with the quality of care and degree of personal attention their families received from midwives. Midwives are trained to manage the care of mothers throughout the period of pregnancy and childbirth, and serve both mothers and newborns after birth. This continuity puts the midwife in a unique position to support the family in the often difficult postpartum period. Midwives view childbirth within a framework of normality, in contrast to obstetricians whose training is primarily aimed at treating pathology. Midwives do prescribe medication but, as a rule, intervene minimally during labor. Nevertheless, they recognize those conditions that require a physician's expertise or the special complications that require transferring the mother to a hospital. (States vary in their licensing and regulation of midwives. In some states midwives can practice only in hospitals, while in others they can practice only outside hospitals.)

The feelings expressed by the five men in this chapter were representative of the wider group of participating fathers whom we interviewed. Many, like Jack, first became involved in the birth process as a result of their partners' requests. Others, like Brian, attributed their participation to their own personal desires which often coincided happily with their partners' preferences. For some men the decision to be present throughout labor and delivery was an easy one; for others, it represented a difficult and sometimes awkward grappling with the realization that they were involving themselves in the "alien" world of childbirth. There were men who found the experience exhilarating; others viewed it as a demanding ordeal. All expressed overwhelming relief at the moment their babies were born. These five men did have one more thing in common: they were able to take themselves a crucial step beyond their own concerns. Their styles and their approaches may have differed, but each man had the deep satisfaction of having been with his partner during their child's birth.

CHAPTER SEVEN

Labor and Birth

If you have decided to assist your partner during labor and the birth of your child, you probably have only vague notions about what you will be doing. No one can supply a scenario or tell you exactly how you feel because no one can predict how your partner's labor will progress and what her needs will be. However, even though each couple's experience is a unique combination of many possibilities, most labors and deliveries typically include a standard sequence of events. We will describe that sequence here, including a rundown of the typical activities of childbirth coaches to give you an idea of what to expect.

Because most births in this country still take place in traditional hospital settings, our discussion centers on that kind of setting, If you are having your baby at home or in a birthing room or maternity center, your role as coach will be the same, although the effects of the environment on you and your partner will be different.

FALSE LABOR

During the final weeks of pregnancy, your partner may experience several episodes of "false labor" also called Braxton-Hicks contractions. False labor contractions differ from real contractions in a number of ways: (1) they usually are not regular; (2) they last for a long time; (3) they stop or change character if the woman changes her position or walks around; and (4) they do not increase in intensity or cause any changes in the cervix.

Braxton-Hicks contractions begin in the early months of pregnancy, although at that time the woman cannot sense the rhythmic hardening and softening of the uterus. With time these contractions become stronger and may cause distress and discomfort. Some couples interpret these contractions as the onset of labor and race off to the hospital, only to be turned around and sent home.

Frequent episodes of false labor can take their toll on you and your partner, causing you both undue concern and fatigue. You may want to suggest the following comfort measures and participate with her in some of them: a change in position, a short walk, the use of a heating pad or cold pack on her back (because temperature changes decrease sensation), a good massage, pelvic rocking exercises, a warm shower or bath, or a glass of wine or beer to promote relaxation.

Because you will want to be able to analyze contractions during real labor, you can learn what a contraction feels like by analyzing Braxton-Hicks contractions. Remember the uterus is a large muscle. Its contractions cause the lowermost portion, the cervix, to thin out (efface) and open (dilate). You might think of the process in terms of the interaction between your head and your turtleneck sweater. In order for your head to go through the small ribbed opening, the neck of the sweater must widen and shorten. The fetus can move into the vagina or birth canal only after the cervix is fully effaced and fully dilated.

To feel contractions, place your hand on your partner's abdomen just below her navel. When a contraction begins you should feel her uterus harden, almost like your biceps hardens when you make a fist. The movement of a contraction is similar to a wave. It grows hard slowly, reaches a peak, and then softens slowly. The hardening also shifts its location along her uterus, beginning at the top (fundus) and moving downward.

THE SEQUENCE OF LABOR

Real labor is divided into three stages. Stage I spans cervical dilation from its beginning until it is complete (to ten centimeters). Stage II spans the time from complete dilation until the infant is born. Stage III marks the time from the birth of the baby to the delivery of the afterbirth (placenta).

Stage I is the longest period and is the time most often referred to as labor. This stage is divided into three phases based on the extent of dilation: Phase I (0–3 centimeters dilated) is called Early Labor; Phase II (3–7 centimeters dilated) is called Active Labor; and Phase III (7–10 centimeters dilated) is called Transition.

WHEN LABOR STARTS

For each woman, labor begins in a different way. In fact, any one woman's different labors may begin differently. For some women labor begins with real contractions. Others first notice a pinkish mucous discharge (called the bloody show). Contractions and bloody show both increase as labor progresses.

In some labors, the onset of contractions is immediately preceded by the breaking of the amniotic sac (the bag of waters). Sometimes this is called the rupturing of the membranes. If the bag of waters breaks, there may or may not be a gush of fluids. In any case, your partner probably will leak fluid continuously until the baby is born. To protect your mattress, put an old shower curtain or plastic sheet under your bed linen during the last few weeks of pregnancy; to protect your car and other furniture, cover seat cushions with a towel. (Remember, leakage of fluid from the vagina anytime during the pregnancy is something you should report to your doctor or midwife.)

Most first-time couples question whether or not these beginning contractions are the "real thing." When in doubt, an examination by your health care provider either in his or her office or at the hospital can reveal whether or not labor has actually begun. During the initial admission exam your partner may be experiencing contractions, so it is wise to remain with her and offer guidance and help with breathing and relaxation. Just being with her and holding her hand during the exam is a way of saying, "I'm here. We'll do this together. You're great. Everything will be okay."

Even if your partner's contractions are diagnosed as genuine, they may be widely spaced and irregular, or an internal examination may show that effacement and dilation have not progressed sufficiently to warrant her being admitted to the hospital at that time. In that case, you both may be sent home to wait for the contractions to come in a more regular pattern and at a shorter interval.

PHASE I: EARLY LABOR

If your partner is having her first baby, labor may last twelve to fourteen hours. At the very beginning of labor, contractions are usually fifteen to twenty minutes apart. That is, there is a span of fifteen to twenty minutes between the beginning of one contraction and the beginning of the next one. Most early labor contractions are said to be weak, although for your partner they may be powerful and unlike anything she has ever felt. Each contraction may last thirty-five to forty seconds. In active labor (Phase II), contractions are stronger, more frequent (coming as close as one and one-half to two minutes apart), and may last as long as seventy to ninety seconds. Strong, regular contractions, while less easy to adapt to, usually accompany a rapidly progressing labor. Weak, irregular contractions may indicate a prolonged labor.

The period of early labor is usually spent at home. During this phase you and your partner should both try to rest, hard as that may be under the circumstances. However, if you remind yourselves that hard labor is ahead for both of you, you will realize that your best efforts can be made if you start out rested. If possible, get back in bed together, or if the bag of waters is still intact, take a warm bath or shower together. At this point it is too late to worry about your list of "things-to-do before the baby comes." No new baby has ever complained about a room without curtains or an incomplete wardrobe.

Sometimes, women are told not to eat or drink while in labor, but this prohibition does not apply to the expectant father. It is important that you eat something now, while you have the chance. Choose something you like and that will sustain you for a long time. Your partner should eat lightly, avoiding fatty foods and foods containing milk.These foods are difficult to digest and could cause nausea and vomiting in labor when the digestive system slows down. A full stomach can be particularly dangerous for a woman who must be given a general anesthetic. If your partner declines to eat, do not let her go too long without fluids. The best nourishment comes from fluids containing carbohydrates, such as tea with honey or jelly, light soups, and Jello.

If your partner is beginning to feel physical discomfort, she will need your support and love more than ever. First-time mothers who have never experienced labor may become frightened and tense as the contractions increase in intensity and frequency. You are the person most important to her, the one who can find the right words to help her relax. In addition, your hands can be a great source of comfort to your partner through stroking, hugging, and massaging.

Don't feel discouraged if your partner does not communicate how much she appreciates your help; it is not uncommon for laboring women to become relatively uncommunicative. You may have to ask her how you can best help her get through this phase. She may find it easier to answer specific questions than to express more abstract feelings. One mother put it this way:

> *I remember feeling silly. On the one hand I wanted John to rub my back, but as soon as he touched me I became annoyed. It was almost as if I couldn't express to him what I really wanted. I really was pleased that*

he was with me, but I was getting so "into" my role as a laboring woman that I couldn't relate to him the way I usually did.

While consumption of alcohol is not recommended during pregnancy, a glass of wine in early labor may give both of you a sense of well-being and comfort. Even though your partner is the one experiencing the apparent physiological changes, you are likely to be excited and tense, even upset or panicky. It is important that you, too, concentrate on relaxing.

You should time contractions intermittently during early labor. Try to feel the contractions for yourself, and ask your partner to confirm that the contractions are beginning and ending when you think they are. You will need to keep a record of when each contraction begins and subsides (see page 122). From these two figures, you can determine the duration of each contraction and the interval between contractions. You have probably been told to alert your midwife or doctor when the contractions are five to seven minutes apart. If for any reason you feel uncomfortable about waiting this long, do not hesitate to phone earlier.

When you and your partner decide to call the midwife or obstetrician, be prepared to answer the following questions:

(1) How close are the contractions?
(2) How long do they last?
(3) Are they strong?
(4) What measures have you found successful in decreasing or alleviating the pain?

Based on your answers to these questions, your birth attendant will tell you to call back with a later report or have you go to the hospital. (In the case of a home birth, the attendant may prepare to come to your house.)

The realization that birth is near is at once frightening and thrilling. It is very likely that within twenty-four hours you will be a parent. If the enormity of the event to come hasn't hit you before, it may hit you now. As you and your partner embark on what is likely to be an exhausting experience, try to remember that the processes of labor and birth do not last forever, and that all efforts are well repaid. No other work will ever give you such a feeling of total fulfillment.

Timing Contractions

You might want to use the following format when keeping a record of your partner's contractions. In the lefthand column jot down the exact time each contraction begins. In the second column indicate how many seconds that contraction lasts. In the third column indicate the interval between the beginning of that contraction and the beginning of the one that preceded it. Use the fourth column for notes or comments on the quality of the contraction or your partner's method of coping with it.

Contraction begins	Duration	Interval	Comments
9:20	30 seconds		
9:30	30 seconds	10 minutes	Contractions
9:40	30 seconds	10 minutes	build slowly
9:50	30 seconds	10 minutes	
10:02	30 seconds	12 minutes	
10:14	30 seconds	12 minutes	
10:25	30 seconds	11 minutes	
10:34	35 seconds	9 minutes	
10:44	30 seconds	10 minutes	
10:53	30 seconds	9 minutes	
11:02	35 seconds	9 minutes	
11:11	35 seconds	9 minutes	
⋮	⋮	⋮	

continued on 123

Timing Contractions *continued*

Contraction begins	Duration	Interval	Comments
12:04	45 seconds	6 minutes	Called doctor
12:10	45 seconds	6 minutes	
12:15	60 seconds	5 minutes	Contraction peaking earlier
12:20	50 seconds	5 minutes	
12:25	50 seconds	5 minutes	
12:30	60 seconds	5 minutes	
12:35	60 seconds	5 minutes	Last contraction before drive to hospital
⋮	⋮	⋮	
2:27	75 seconds	4 minutes	Strong contraction
2:31	60 seconds	4 minutes	
2:34	60 seconds	3 minutes	Back labor
2:38	60 seconds	4 minutes	
2:42	75 seconds	4 minutes	
2:45	75 seconds	3 minutes	
2:48	75 seconds	3 minutes	
etc.	etc.	etc.	

You can see that in this hypothetical labor, the beginning contractions come at ten- to twelve-minute intervals and last about half a minute. Within less than two hours, the interval between contractions has decreased to five or six minutes, with each contraction lasting close to a minute. Two hours later, the contractions are coming harder and faster still. The period between contractions is now only three or four minutes long, and the contractions themselves are lasting seventy-five seconds.

PHASE II: ACTIVE LABOR

When your partner's contractions are coming about five to ten minutes apart for at least one hour, she is probably in active labor. About this time, the midwife will be arriving at your house or you will be heading off to the hospital.

One father we spoke to described his hospital journey:

Between contractions I helped Louise move carefully out to the car. She reclined across some towels spread over the back seat, and I got into the driver's seat. It was snowing so I tried to drive slowly and miss the potholes, for if the car jolted I heard it from Louise in the back seat. She was as comfortable as she could be in the midst of having contractions with water leaking. Was I glad I had remembered to put those towels in the car! I figured she must have been far ahead in her labor because she had no interest in talking to me. I tried to calm her down by telling her I loved her and that everything would work out fine. I was glad she didn't see my face because I'm sure I looked more nervous than I tried to sound. I wanted to speed but I didn't dare. We arrived at the hospital safely, but I honestly don't remember seeing a thing along the way except the falling snow and the tail lights of the car in front of us.

The drive to the hospital can be highly stressful for your partner. Stay with her once you arrive. Because she has been moving around, she may need a lot of help relaxing, handling the contractions, and reestablishing breathing patterns. Upon her arrival in the maternity unit, a nurse or doctor will determine whether she is in labor by determining to what degree her cervix is effaced and dilated. This internal examination is done during a contraction and will upset your partner's breathing rhythm, so be prepared to help reestablish it. There is no legitimate reason why you cannot stay with her during this and subsequent internal examinations; in fact, because the examination can be so disruptive, it is important that you be there with her.

If the examination establishes that your partner is not in active labor, she may not be kept in the hospital. Both of you are sure to feel disappointed at this development. That is why it's best not to arrange for her formal admission until after the exam, when you are sure she will be staying. Many hospitals encourage you to fill out an admission form well in advance (usually at the time of the hospital tour) and leave it on file with them. Then, when you are sure your partner will be admitted, you can go to the admissions office to have her form activated. You may want to have a duplicate completed form with you in your bag in case the hospital's filing clerk is a new trainee!

Depending on hospital routine and/or the routines prescribed by your partner's doctor, several procedures may be carried out shortly after admission.

- Blood may be drawn for a blood type determination.
- An intravenous glucose infusion may be started. The glucose gives your partner energy, and the same conduit can be used for introducing other fluids or medication as needed.
- Some of the hair around the vaginal opening may be shaved.
- An enema may be given. Often labor is preceded by diarrhea, nature's own enema. An empty rectum gives the infant maximum space in which to move down the birth canal. An empty rectum also lets a woman feel free to push more forcefully during the second stage of labor without being concerned that she will contaminate the bedclothes and embarrass

herself. After the enema your partner may need a lot of help from you because the enema can increase the intensity of the contractions, and the interruption in her breathing routine may be quite disturbing to her. Do your best to help her regain control and concentration.

- A fetal monitor may be attached to your partner's abdomen. Although the belts or stockinette girdle used to attach the monitor do not interfere with her breathing or relaxation, they will limit her movement. Whenever your partner changes her position, you should call someone to readjust the monitor.

Your partner may discover that it is difficult to find a comfortable position in which to labor. Often the fetal position is the most comfortable (and surely the most appropriate!), because as she rests on her side the weight of the heavy uterus is shifted away from the large blood vessels and spine. Also, when she lies on her side, you will be able to rub her back with greater ease. Use plenty of pillows to support her in a comfortable position. If she is on her side, a pillow placed under her arm and under her uppermost leg will help her relax more muscles.

Remind her to change her position often, especially if the fetus is in a posterior position, with its back resting against her spine and causing back labor. Because she may have difficulty keeping track of time, remind her to shift every half hour. Women with back labor may find some relief by sitting up and leaning forward, by sitting tailor fashion, or by leaning on all fours. The weight of the enlarged uterus is thus shifted forward and off her spine.

Most hospitals do not permit a woman in labor to walk around because of insurance and safety factors. If your partner wants to get out of bed, first obtain permission from the physician or nurse on duty.

When you have a free moment, acquaint yourself with the facilities in the room and those nearby. If you plan to participate in the delivery, find out where you can change into delivery garb and do this early on. As labor progresses, you will have less time to prepare yourself. Ask about the location of the men's room and the public telephone. Be sure to find a chair for yourself; you will be thoroughly exhausted if you remain standing throughout the hours of labor. If you have attended childbirth classes and have brought a bag of special supplies for labor, set these out in a handy place. Find out how to roll the bed up and down and where to get extra pillows, ice chips, a cup, a washcloth, and bed pans and pads. Ask to be shown how to call the nurse and have someone explain how to read the printout generated by the fetal monitor. Get your camera and other delivery room supplies ready.

As your partner goes through Phase II labor, you can be a real help to her by wiping her brow with a cold cloth, feeding her ice chips, massaging her sore back, and applying counterpressure to any bony area of her body against which the fetus is pressing. If you are touching her skin, make sure your hands are warm. Men who have attended childbirth preparation classes know how to coach their partners in rhythmic breathing.

While it is easy enough to perform some of these straightforward, mechanical comfort measures, you may feel you are less successful in satisfying your partner's other often poorly articulated needs. Women in labor frequently become introverted and tune out strangers. As labor progresses, they often can only relate to and communicate with someone very close. You may have to transmit instructions from the nurse or doctor to your partner and relay her needs back to them.

You may be the only one who can effectively help her relax and regulate her breathing.

Since you will never experience labor yourself, you cannot possibly understand all that your partner is going through. Even if she is able to stay on top of her contractions, she is still being poked, examined, touched, and talked about by many different people, most of whom are complete strangers to both of you. How can she possibly feel good about herself as she lies awkward, tired, sore, experiencing some loss of control, with a bloody discharge and fluid leaking from her vagina, wearing a gown that doesn't close, with belts attached to her abdomen and needles in her arms? You will have to be compassionate, understanding, loyal, empathetic, and nondemanding—in other words, a steadfast and selfless supporter. Of course, your job would be a lot easier if the labor were exerting no strain on you. But you, too, will be tense, apprehensive, tired, and unsure. Although you may not be feeling particularly chatty, remember to say "I love you," "You're great," "I'm proud of you," and "I'm glad we're together." These words mean more to a woman in labor than any dose of medication. And such expressions of your devotion will remind both of you that this current bit of hard work is related to your shared lovemaking.

As Phase II labor progresses, you may find that you are feeling tired, bored, or in need of a break. Take a few minutes off and figure out a "comfort measure" for yourself. Get something to eat or drink, make a phone call, watch television, go for a walk, or just relax. Before you leave, tell your partner exactly what you are doing, where you will be, and how long you will be gone. Tell the nurses where you will be in case labor speeds up and birth becomes imminent. *Make sure you return when you said you would.*

Once you return, find out what has happened, whether the contractions have changed, how your partner feels, and whether she has been examined again. If you feel you need another rest period later, take one.

Throughout labor, continue making serious efforts to keep the lines of communication open with both your partner and the maternity staff. Remind your partner that she is doing a fine job, and reassure her that the two of you are working together as a team. Be truthful in your comments to her. Don't be afraid to say, "That really seemed like a hard contraction" or "You're doing great." Let her know that you appreciate how hard she is working. Although you may not get much immediate reinforcement for your efforts or may even begin to feel that you are doing everything wrong, you are probably doing just what is needed, so keep plugging away. After the birth, your partner will be able to tell you that your efforts were crucial to her well-being.

The obstetrician may show up every once in a while to examine your partner during this phase, but you will have more contact with and help from the nurses. Let them know that you rely on them for information and suggestions and that you appreciate their help.

If your partner's labor is not progressing rapidly, the doctor may rupture the bag of waters. This procedure is called an amniotomy and is done with a device that looks like a crochet hook. After an amniotomy the contractions will probably increase both in magnitude and frequency, so be ready to work hard to help your partner reestablish breathing and relaxation patterns. Once her bag of waters is ruptured, whether this occurs spontaneously or not, she should stay in bed. With each contraction she will feel she is leaking fluid. This leaking is uncontrollable because no muscles are working to close the vagina. You may have to change the underpad on her bed frequently or remind the nurse to do so.

PHASE III: TRANSITION

As Phase II labor ends, your partner will enter the phase called transition. Transition is the shortest but most difficult period of labor. The contractions are very long (lasting anywhere from sixty to ninety seconds), very strong, and may come as often as every one and one-half to two minutes. This means your partner has little if any time to rest between contractions. In transition, she will depend on you to recognize when a contraction is subsiding, either by feeling that her uterus is softening or by watching the fetal monitor. If you can reassure her that a contraction is subsiding—even though she cannot feel it herself—she can begin to relax before having to marshal her resources for the next contraction.

During transition the mother may display a number of new physiological symptoms—nausea, vomiting, trembling of the inner thighs and legs, burping, chills, heat spells, and a general feeling of doom. She may begin to feel pressure on her rectum and feel she wants to push or defecate. This is a normal consequence of the infant's head pressing on the rectal muscles. The urge to push may also cause her to tense up, bear down involuntarily, or urinate during a contraction. Her perineum may bulge. However, she should not begin to push until her cervix is completely dilated. The involuntary urge to push is overwhelming and can only be stopped by a conscious effort. Until she has been given the go-ahead to push, your partner should fight off the urge by blowing outward with great force, as if she were trying to blow up a balloon. A person cannot blow out and bear down at the same time. Try it.

The contractions of transition are often so overwhelming that your partner may completely lose her ability to concentrate on her breathing. If this happens, breathe with her to help her sustain the rhythm needed to stay in control. This may be the most helpful thing you will do during labor, so make sure you know the breathing patterns thoroughly. If you are standing at her side and breathing energetically, you may find yourself getting lightheaded or feel your lips tingling. These are signs that you are hyperventilating. Sit down for a few moments and breathe into your cupped hands or into a paper bag until you feel better. It also helps to put your head down between your knees.

Many women become paranoid and discouraged during transition. They feel they are not making progress, that labor will never end, and so on. Often it is during transition that the woman who planned an unmedicated delivery feels she can no longer cope without medication. Her expressions of anger, pain, unhappiness, and resignation will frighten you. No one likes to stand by while another person is in pain, especially if that person is someone he loves. Try to calm down. After all, you knew this might happen. As terrible as you feel, take some comfort in the fact that these terrible feelings are signals that the birth is very near. Now you must reconcile the conflicting signals from your heart and your mind. You will have to help her make the right decision at a most difficult time. Does your partner really want anesthesia? Does she really want to lose the sensations associated with birth? Will she regret, in the days and months to come, not feeling or seeing the birth of her baby? Do you know what your partner really wants?

If you find yourself in this very difficult situation, pause for a moment while you collect yourself. Then say to her,

"Let's try to make it through one more contraction." Each "one more contraction" brings you closer to your child's birth. Eventually, one of those strong contractions will open her cervix to ten centimeters. Remind her of this, and remind yourself as well! This ability to narrow your thoughts to include only the most immediate events will be critical to getting both of you through this difficult period.

As your partner succeeds in getting through each contraction, she may be able to pull herself back together. If medication must be used, try not to get lost in feelings of guilt or disappointment. If the medication is used judiciously, you will be able to continue with a prepared childbirth. The medication may, in fact, help your partner regain control of her contractions. This control is the essential factor in prepared childbirth.

The cervix dilates rapidly during transition, so call the doctor, midwife, or nurse, and ask to have your partner examined. Once the cervix is dilated to ten centimeters, the doctor will give her permission to begin pushing the baby through the birth canal. Stage II labor has begun.

As soon as your partner begins to push, she will probably feel some relief. Remind her that the baby is about to emerge. She may also feel optimistic now, knowing that she is pushing the baby down the birth canal. By pushing, she is working with the contractions instead of holding them back. The contractions will change during this period of pushing, often slowing down to intervals of two to three minutes. If she has received a regional anesthetic (an epidural or a caudal block), she may not consciously feel the urge to push. The doctor and nurses will have to assist her by giving her a signal to bear down.

The most natural position to take for birth is with legs drawn up to shorten the pelvis. In this position—whether on one's back or squatting—the pelvis is tilted, the legs are wide apart, and the vagina is spread open. If the woman takes a squatting position, the force exerted by gravity will help pull the baby down the birth canal. You can help your partner get into a squatting position by rolling up the bed or propping her up with pillows. Your partner can shorten her pelvis by holding her thighs close to her abdomen. This will give the baby more room to maneuver downward toward the vagina. You may have to support one or both of your partner's legs during pushing. If a nurse is present, you may each support one leg, or one of you may support her shoulders while the other holds her legs.

Again you will be working with the contractions. Between contractions, have your partner close her eyes and rest. This brief rest period between contractions gives her a chance to renew her energy. If this is her first baby, she may have to push for one to two hours. If this is not her first baby, and her pushing is very effective, she may be taken to the delivery room to push there. Sometimes the doctor may ask that your partner stop pushing for a moment. In this case, she should once again blow out forcefully a few times to inhibit the urge to push down. Sometimes a woman is asked to breathe through an oxygen mask during contractions. This helps saturate the baby's blood with oxygen during the contraction. In no way does it interfere with pushing.

Sometimes your first view of the baby is a patch of matted hair. With each push the baby advances two steps and retreats one. If you have brought a mirror in your delivery bag and are still in the labor room, hold the mirror in such a way that your partner can see how much of the baby's head is visible. Seeing evidence that a real baby is on its way is exhilarating and will give both you and your partner a new burst of energy.

BIRTH

If you are in a traditional hospital, your partner will be moved to the delivery room either on her labor bed or on a stretcher. When you leave the labor room, take a pillow to prop up her back, your camera or recording equipment, and a cold washcloth. Above all, don't forget her eyeglasses.

In the delivery room, you will stand or sit near your partner's head. The nurse will put her legs in stirrups and scrub the perineal area with surgical soap. Sterile sheets will be draped around her legs, thighs, and over her abdomen. No one is supposed to touch these drapes; you may hold your partner's hand under the drapes. A mirror on the ceiling will be adjusted so that both of you can watch the birth. Your partner may be unnerved to look in the mirror and see that her face is somewhat purple, a result of broken blood vessels from all that pushing. Tell her to concentrate instead on the action down below! (Her coloring will be back to normal by the next day.)

At this point the birth is imminent and you will be feeling quite positive. You and your partner will also be getting a lot of encouragement from the other people in the delivery room. Almost everyone is affected by the excitement of birth. There will usually be at least one nurse, your birth attendant, and a staff pediatrician in the delivery room. Everyone present, except your partner, will be wearing a surgical mask, but you will be able to tell who is who! (Some of these sterility conditions should be carried out even if you are having your baby at home.)

The obstetrician will start running the show at this point. If he or she is softspoken, you may have to repeat any instructions for your partner. Often the obstetrician makes a controlled incision in the area between the vagina and the anus. This is called an episiotomy. It enlarges the opening of the birth canal and makes it less likely that your partner's tissue will tear as the baby emerges. If you see quite a lot of blood in the mirror, do not be alarmed; this is normal.

The vagina and perineum are very elastic; they can and will stretch a great deal in the next few minutes. When the baby's head is ready to be delivered, the obstetrician or midwife will say, "Blow out with the next contraction. Do not push." This is done because it is best to deliver the head between contractions when there is little pressure against the baby's soft skull. Steady yourself. This is the moment you've both been working toward. You're about to get your first look at your new child. As soon as the head is eased out, your partner should feel some relief, as the largest part of the infant is no longer in her vagina. At this point, the doctor or midwife may suction mucous from the baby's mouth and nose to remove the secretions that remain from its trip through the birth canal. The baby's head may appear blue; this is common.

With the next contraction, as the shoulders and the rest of the body appear, you and your partner will have your first complete look at your baby. The baby's bluish skin will quickly turn pink. He or she may be wrinkled, wet, and covered with bloody mucous or a cheesy substance called vernix. No matter—the baby will still look absolutely beautiful to you. He or she may be crying. You may be crying yourself.

These first few moments following birth are charged with emotion. Fathers seem to have a unique feeling at this time. You may have been working for hours to support your partner, not feeling any physical discomfort but experiencing strong emotional discomfort in watching the sometimes grueling work of labor and delivery. Now, finally, you can release all your pent-up emotions. It is okay to cry, laugh, sigh, kiss your partner, yell "Yippee!" or anything else that makes you feel good. At the moment of birth some fathers are so stunned that they just stare at their newborn without saying a word. One father recalled his impressions:

> *I thought I was prepared. I attended all the classes, I practiced with Ruth every night, and I read everything I could. But do you know, I never expected this to be so beautiful. It is such a miracle. I felt as though I was floating on a cloud. Nothing prepared me for the exhilaration of the actual birth.*

Some fathers and mothers are surprised at the appearance of their infant. What does a new baby look like? Are they really cute? beautiful? A newborn baby is wet, wrinkled, and wiggly. Its head may be slightly elongated from the long process of moving through the birth canal. Its hair is matted with blood and vernix (a cheesey white substance that protects the infant *in utero*). Fingers and hands may shake uncontrollably as the infant is brought into the cold air of the delivery room. Eyes are usually wrinkled up, although some new babies open their eyes and begin to look around. The umbilical cord is whitish yellow, about the diameter of your thumb.

As mentioned earlier, some babies are slightly blue for the first few moments until they begin to cry and pink up. Sometimes, hands and feet remain bluish for several days until the baby's circulation is well established. Don't be alarmed if your baby's ears or legs or toes seem slightly misshapen. Just think how your raincoat would look after being tightly packed in a suitcase for nine months! You would expect a rumpled sleeve, a twisted lapel. Your baby's "irregularities" will no doubt disappear in a day or two—just don't try to steam them out in the shower!

As soon as your newborn is delivered, the main goal of the obstetric team is to ensure that the baby is healthy and breathing well. All babies receive their initial screening via the Apgar score (see page 139). The Apgar score provides the delivery room staff with an instant appraisal of the infant's condition, including the heartrate and neurological functioning and can indicate need for follow-up in the newborn nursery. This assessment is done by the attending pediatrician or pediatric nurse at one minute and again at five minutes after birth. The Apgar score rates your infant on general appearance, heartrate, reflexes, activity level, and respiration. Each area is given a score from zero to two, with a possible combined score reaching ten points. One father we know kept asking, "What's his score? What's his score?" as though he were at a football game. It is wise to remember that most infants are not a "ten" at birth, so don't be alarmed if your baby's initial score is off by one or two points.

Sometimes the infant is placed on the mother's stomach before the unbilical cord is cut. The parents can then feel their new baby still warm and wet. Early bonding is begun here. The timing for cutting the cord depends on the attending physician. After the cord is cut, a small plastic clamp is placed about one inch from your baby's umbilicus. This clamp will remain in place until the cord stump dries up and falls off, usually in five to seven days.

As soon as the cord is cut, the baby is wrapped in a warm towel and taken to a warmer-crib in the delivery room for its five-minute Apgar assessment. You are free to walk around the delivery room, and you will no doubt find that your attention is divided between your partner and your baby. Your partner must now continue to push until the placenta (afterbirth) has been delivered. This third and final stage of labor can take up to thirty minutes. When the entire placenta has been delivered and any lacerations have been repaired, the obstetrician will stitch together your partner's episiotomy.

In the meantime, your baby has been cleaned up, weighed, measured, given a hospital tag, footprinted, and wrapped in a warm blanket. Silver nitrate drops are put in the baby's eyes at this time. This procedure is regulated by state laws and protects the baby from blindness caused by an organism present in the woman's birth canal if she has gonorrhea. (If you wish, you may be able to delay this last procedure for an hour or two so your baby will be able to see you clearly and not through a silver nitrate haze.)

You and your partner will always remember the first time you hold your baby. It is truly a moment to cherish. If you are feeling shaky, sit down. Your partner may be feeling shaky too, but she can hold the baby even though she is still on the delivery table. It is hard to predict exactly what your baby might be doing—moving with random jerky motions, staring wide-eyed, struggling to open its eyes, crying, or lying very still. Remember, your infant has just been thrust from its snug, warm, dark, wet environment into a bright, cold, dry, noisy room. It is an extremely dramatic change. Hold your baby close and give it as much warmth and love and protection as you can.

Congratulations, Dad! You made it! You're a FATHER!

Apgar Score

	0	1	2
Heartrate	Absent	Under 100 per minute	Over 100 per minute
Respiratory Effort	Absent	Slow, gasping	Good, strong cry
Muscle Tone	Flaccid	Poor	Active motion
Reflexes	No response	Grimace, some response	Active, crying
Color	Body pale or blue	Body pink, extremities blue	Completely pink

CHAPTER EIGHT

Unexpected Events

It is very difficult to prepare oneself for an unexpected turn of events. However, too often an unanticipated development that is not inherently negative becomes a serious problem for couples who are uninformed and/or rigid in their thinking. As a father-to-be, you may not relish the prospect of focusing your already apprehensive thoughts on events that might complicate your partner's labor and your child's birth. Still, you may find that any "complications" that do occur will seem less overwhelming if you prime yourself now for the unexpected.

UNEXPECTED EVENTS DURING THE NINTH MONTH

Let's backtrack a moment and consider some problems frequently associated with the last month of pregnancy.

Edema (Fluid Retention)

Toward the end of pregnancy, and especially in hot weather, a pregnant women may experience edema or fluid retention in her face and extremities. Shoes and rings may not fit, and her face may appear puffy. She can help lessen these symptoms by cutting back on excess salt intake and resting during the day. If edema occurs suddenly or increases markedly, notify your physician or midwife, as these might be warning signs of toxemia (pre-eclampsia).

Pre-eclampsia (Toxemia)

Pre-eclampsia is a mysterious condition of late pregnancy expressed as high blood pressure, protein excretion in the urine, and swelling of the ankles, hands, and face. It is potentially harmful to both mother and baby and should be treated as soon as possible. Treatment may include bedrest at home, tranquilizers, or even hospitalization. Regular prenatal checkups are very important for the early detection of problems associated with pre-eclampsia.

Bedrest

If your partner needs complete or partial bedrest for any reason, you may have to assume a major role in running the household. If you are unable to keep up with the shopping, cooking, laundry, and other maintenance chores in addition to working full-time and being a companion to your partner, raise the white flag and ask for help from relatives, friends, and coworkers. If your partner senses that the household is "falling apart" around her, she will feel uncomfortable staying in bed. Give her your encouragement and support so she can stay in bed with peace of mind.

Pregnancy Extending Past Due Date

If your partner is past her due date or if the baby does not seem to be continuing to grow, the physician or midwife will be monitoring her estriol level as an indicator of placental function. If the estriol level falls, the physician or midwife may recommend nonstress tests, stress tests, or induction (see pages 69, 70, 143).

Bleeding

Bleeding may occur anytime during pregnancy. Bleeding is not normal, and if it should occur, notify your doctor or midwife immediately. A number of conditions may cause bleeding at different times during pregnancy. One of the most common causes of bleeding late in pregnancy is placenta previa (see Glossary).

Spotting, in contrast to bleeding, usually is not a cause for alarm. Unlike bleeding, which looks like menstrual flow, spotting consists of a discharge of a few drops of blood, usually detected on underwear or toilet tissue. Your partner may spot after vaginal examination by the doctor, after intercourse, or after the mucous plug has been lost (a sign that labor may be starting).

Induction

If the doctor or midwife wishes to induce labor, there are a number of ways that labor can be started. Sometimes an enema does the trick. If the cervix is partially dilated, labor may be induced by rupturing the bag of waters. Commonly, the synthetic hormone Pitocin (given orally, by lozenge, or intravenously) is used to stimulate uterine contractions. When Pitocin is administered intravenously, the rate of contractions is controlled by raising or lowering the number of drops given per minute. Pitocin-induced contractions tend to peak sooner and last longer than natural contractions, but the stages of labor are exactly the same as in any labor. Thus, if your partner is induced, she will still experience early labor, active labor, and transition labor, though these phases may progress more quickly.

Premature Birth

When labor begins before the fetus is fully mature, the baby may be small and predisposed to many complications. Small and/or sick babies may have to be transferred to an intensive care nursery for observation and care. Although you can take comfort in the fact that most "preemies" grow up showing no lingering signs of their premature arrival, the first few days or weeks of a premature baby's life can be frightening.

The father often has a special role to play in the case of a premature baby since he can accompany the baby to the nursery, see how the baby will be cared for, talk to the nurses and physicians about the baby's condition, and carry this information back to his partner. Until the mother feels well enough to visit the nursery on her own, the father is the communication line between her and baby. Even after the mother can visit the baby in the nursery, most hospitals encourage *both* parents to spend time with the baby.

It is common for the premature infant to remain in the hospital's intensive care nursery even after the mother has been allowed to return home. This can be an anxious and upsetting event for both parents, since it is the expectation of every pregnant couple to leave the hospital with their baby in their arms. Be reassured that your infant will be receiving round-the-clock care in the hospital's nursery and that she or he will be released into your care as soon as possible. Many hospitals allow you to remain with your baby most of the day, and you should do this if you can. It is important that your baby get to know its parents as soon as possible.

On a related point, it is important that both you and your partner understand the premature baby's critical need for mother's milk. Many neonatologists advocate that mothers try to express breast milk to bring to their hospitalized babies. If your partner becomes tired or disenchanted by this "long distance" feeding process, you may need to encourage her in this effort.

UNEXPECTED EVENTS DURING LABOR

The Elements

Whether or not it is true that most labors start with the full moon or during a storm, many expectant parents have to fight Mother Nature to get to the hospital. You should have contingency plans in the event there is a torrential downpour or a twenty-four-inch snowfall when your partner goes into labor. Remember, the police or rescue squad will usually be glad to assist you if you need help.

As your partner's due date approaches, it is a good idea to make a timed run-through of the trip to the hospital. Be sure you know alternative routes in case of heavy traffic or bad weather. Also, to make the trip to the hospital smooth—

- keep a full tank of gas;
- park your car in a consistent spot near your home;
- have an extra set of car keys;
- have your hospital bags packed a few weeks in advance;
- keep loose change in your pocket;
- leave word as to where you can be reached if you are not at your place of work.

Change in Father Participation Plans

Due to unforeseen circumstances, a father may be excluded from a birth that he had wanted to attend or included when he did not expect to be. No one can predict the course of labor, and you cannot get an iron-clad guarantee that your participation requests will be adhered to. Remain flexible and understanding regardless of the circumstances. Do your homework ahead of time and check with the doctor and hospital to see what their policies are if something unexpected happens (see Appendix I).

The Absent Birth Attendant

Your carefully chosen birth attendant may be unavailable when your baby decides to arrive. When the midwife or physician you have selected announces vacation or conference plans, be sure you and your partner both meet the substitute who has been selected to assist at the birth. Although you may feel awkward in knowing that a relative stranger will deliver your baby, you need to trust your original doctor's or midwife's judgment in choosing this substitute. Most obstetrical practices have two or three members to avoid the last-minute entry of a stranger.

You As the Lone Birth Attendant

When a baby is born enroute to the hospital or before the midwife arrives at your home, the birth is often easy and uncomplicated. *The Emergency Birth Manual* describes the procedures you should carry out in order to maximize maternal and infant safety. If you learn these procedures, you will be better prepared for your part in such an unlikely, but not impossible, emergency.

The manual suggests you let the baby deliver itself. Then put the infant on its mother's abdomen and bundle the two together. Let the cord dangle without tying it off, and place the placenta lower than the mother (preferably in a container or plastic bag so the doctor or midwife can examine it later). Encourage your partner to nurse the baby immediately, even if she had no intention of doing so since this helps reduce maternal bleeding. If the baby is not breathing, place its head at an angle lower than its body to encourage excess mucous to drain, and then gently slap the baby's hands and feet.

Trembling

Your partner may "shake like a leaf" at many points in labor, but this occurs most often at the very beginning and at the very end. You may be alarmed to see your calm, cool, collected partner trembling from head to toe. Trembling is another normal accompaniment of labor and will go away eventually. When it occurs, remember that a few kind words and a warm hug will help a lot.

Nausea and Vomiting

As labor begins, your partner's digestive system stops functioning. This, in addition to her excitement, may lead to nausea and vomiting. To reduce the chance of suffering from nausea, your partner should eat lightly once labor begins—preferably clear fluids, Jello, or light foods such as toast or applesauce. Milk products or fatty foods should be avoided as they take a long time to digest and tend to cause nausea. Some physicians recommend that your partner not eat or drink anything once labor has begun. Remember to discuss this topic during prenatal visits to the doctor.

Nausea and Lightheadedness

These symptoms may strike you, the father-to-be, at some point in labor. Many factors may cause you to be momentarily overcome by nausea or dizziness—the excitement of the situation, the newness of the surroundings, the temperature of the labor room, the fact that you haven't eaten for many hours, and so on. This is not a time to be brave or act embarrassed; rather, pay attention to your body signals. Sit down on a nearby chair or the floor if you have to, and put your head between your legs. The nurse may offer you an ammonia ampule to sniff; this will help clear your head.

Prevention is the best way to deal with this normal but unexpected event.

- Wear relatively lightweight clothes to the labor and delivery room, even if it is winter. The labor room is usually warm because the temperature is adjusted to suit a woman wearing a flimsy hospital gown.
- Make sure the labor room has adequate ventilation. If the room feels stuffy, ask if you may open a window or door.
- Eat a well-balanced snack or meal before coming to the hospital. If your snack is high in protein, it will be digested slowly and will therefore keep your blood sugar level fairly even for a long period of time. If you grab a candy bar on the way out the door, your blood sugar level will rise momentarily but will drop quickly.
- Pack a nutritious snack to take along to the hospital. If you bring some raisins and nuts or peanut butter crackers, these will keep your blood sugar level up and help you avoid the dizzy feeling that accompanies low blood sugar. Be sure not to eat in front of your partner if she is feeling hungry or nauseated.
- Take periodic breaks from the labor room. You should allow yourself a bathroom-stretch break every few hours during the early part of labor to

keep yourself alert and comfortable. Remember, once your partner enters the more active and demanding phases of labor, both of you will be reluctant to be separated for any reason.

- If you are not feeling well, tell the nurse. Often the nurse will be able to suggest something to make you feel better, whether it is a glass of ice water or a bed to lie down on for a few minutes. Most family-oriented nurses are concerned that you remain comfortable during labor.

Medication

Medication is often a valuable tool that can help a woman proceed with a long or painful delivery. Its use during childbirth, though often unwanted, is sometimes required. On the other hand, sometimes a woman who planned on a medicated birth finds that labor is proceeding so smoothly that medication becomes unnecessary. You and your partner should consider both kinds of possibilities.

There are many types of medication offered in labor. Be sure to discuss the advantages and disadvantages and the indication for each type with your physician or midwife during prenatal examinations. It is not easy and sometimes not even possible to discuss medication in the midst of hard labor.

Forceps Delivery

"Low" forceps are used to assist the baby down the vaginal canal when the mother cannot push effectively. This can occur when the mother is exhausted or when medication interferes with her sensations. The forceps often leave marks on the baby's head, but generally these disappear in a few days. The very dangerous process of using "high" forceps is no longer practiced. In this procedure, forceps were used to pull the baby out of the uterus itself.

Unexpected Vaginal Delivery

Sometimes a woman expects her baby to be born by cesarean delivery, and she and her partner do not prepare for a vaginal delivery. The candidates for this kind of surprise include women who have been told their pelvises are not large enough to accommodate the infant's head, those who have had previous babies by cesarean delivery, or those who had elected cesarean deliveries. The couple can be prepared for such a surprise by participating in prepared childbirth classes on the odd chance that their baby will choose to find its own way out without surgical intervention.

Fetal Distress

The fetal heart rate is measured frequently, sometimes constantly, during labor and delivery. Diverse conditions that threaten the well-being of the fetus are reflected in changes in the fetal heart rate. The normal rate is 120 to 160 beats per minute, twice the adult heart rate. Fetal distress is usually interpreted from a pattern of slowed heart rate, although there are some conditions in which distress can lead to a very fast heart rate. Fetal distress may reflect a number of problems, including: (1) excess pressure on the baby's head (often seen transiently during the pushing phase of labor); (2) the umbilical cord being wrapped around the baby's neck or body; (3) insufficient blood supply coming through the placenta; (4) some type of maternal illness.

If distress is suspected, your partner may be asked to turn on her left side to facilitate circulation. She may also be given oxygen and intravenous fluids. If the distress does not clear up, the physician may recommend a cesarean delivery.

CESAREAN BIRTH

There has been a significant rise in the number of cesarean deliveries that occur as unexpected events during labor. Since the cesarean delivery rate is climbing to almost twenty percent across the country, this topic is presented in considerable detail. We have also included a case history to give you more background and a fuller understanding of what could occur if your partner experiences a cesarean delivery.

A cesarean birth is the delivery of the baby through a surgical incision in the mother's abdomen and uterus. The incision passes through the layers of skin, the subcutaneous fat tissue, the abdominal muscle, and the peritoneum. Once the large purple uterus can be seen, a small transverse incision is made, and there is a great gush of amniotic fluid. The incision is often no larger than ten centimeters, the size of a completely dilated cervix. The baby is usually removed head first through this small incision. This delivery is accomplished within a few minutes; more time is spent after a cesarean birth to repair the mother's tissues.

A cesearean delivery may be a scheduled procedure, it may be done as an emergency, or it may be performed as a last recourse to deliver a baby who cannot be delivered vaginally due to its position or due to its mother's lack of progress in labor. Often the decision to perform a cesarean is made under critical circumstances, when either the infant or mother is in distress, or when it becomes evident that the pelvis is too narrow to accommodate the baby's head. When a cesarean is done for fetal distress, the nurses and doctors seem to fly, so don't be alarmed if you are ignored or asked to step out of the room. In cases of distress, when speed is critical, the mother may be given a general anesthetic; if more time is available, a regional anesthetic (usually a saddle block or epidural) may be preferred. Under regional anesthesia, many women feel the pull of the infant as it is being delivered, although they rarely experience pain.

As with vaginal deliveries, the cesarean birth experience can lend itself to a variety of approaches. The type of anesthesia used, the type of incision made, and the type of postpartum medication available are all issues that should be discussed with your physician before delivery.

Some hospitals are now allowing expectant fathers to witness their child's birth by cesarean, usually if they have attended special preparatory classes. Couples who know that their child will be delivered by cesarean, or couples who find themselves in a high or moderate risk category in their pregnancy, may find it worthwhile to attend classes because they provide information, support, and advice related to their specific needs. In any case, you and your partner should discuss ahead of time whether you want to be present at a cesarean birth should one be indicated in your case. Be sure you make an early and complete investigation of your hospital's policy on this issue (see Appendix I).

The experience of one couple, Jeff and Michele, may suggest some issues worth considering during pregnancy.

Jeff and Michele: The Emergency Cesarean Delivery

Jeff and Michele had prepared enthusiastically for their first child's birth. They had attended childbirth classes and had practiced the relaxation and breathing techniques conscientiously. Arrangements were made with their doctor and the hospital staff to have a Leboyer delivery and to take pictures in the delivery room.

During labor, however, a vaginal examination indicated that Michele's pelvis was small, and x-rays confirmed that the baby's head was too large to pass through the pelvis. The doctor arranged for her to have an epidural, and he prepared to perform a cesarean delivery.

Jeff stayed with Michele for the half-hour that was needed before the epidural took effect. Jeff spent this time trying to reassure Michele that a Lamaze Leboyer delivery was not as important as the safe birth of the baby. Besides, he reassured her he would be all right waiting outside the delivery room. Michele was saddened by the prospect of not giving birth to their baby as they had practiced, and she was upset that Jeff wouldn't be in the delivery room with her. Jeff's initial reaction was two-pronged. First, he felt disappointed that their original plans had been "cancelled." Second, he felt somewhat elated knowing that their baby would be born within the hour. In his own words, "Suddenly, all the uncertainty of labor was gone."

When Michele was taken into the delivery room, Jeff went to the waiting room. "I avoided pacing," he remembered, "but it was a slow forty-five minutes. I couldn't concentrate on anything. I was in a fog, in a state of limbo. I really hadn't adjusted to being left out of things."

Twenty minutes after their daugher's birth, Jeff saw the baby and this began to remedy his disorientation. Nevertheless, he reported that for several days he had to reassure Michele about the experience. She was still depressed over the fact that they hadn't been together for the birth. "Michele really needed help right after the operation," he confided. "It was hard on her emotionally and physically. My own feelings had to wait. Maybe that was good, because as time passed those feelings probably became less intense. Still, eventually I had to work on myself. I had missed out on an important event. I guess I'll always feel some regret."

Jeff and Michele's experience points out that there is a growing population of men who want to be with their partners for childbirth but are excluded when their physician determines that a cesarean delivery is necessary. Most fathers we talked to explained that they were not psychologically prepared for this possibility, even though the procedure and the reasons that might make it necessary had been explained in their childbirth classes. Most expectant fathers had put their energies into preparing for a vaginal birth. One man commented that the information about cesarean births had been directed at the women; no recommendations had been made to the men as to how they might deal with their feelings if they found themselves excluded from the birth for which they had prepared so rigorously.

One father whose wife was given general anesthesia for cesarean birth related how he spent time with the baby in the nursery immediately after birth. He was with the infant for an hour and a half, during which time he touched and cuddled him. "I wanted to be there to deal with the baby," he said. "I figured the doctor would take care of my wife while she was coming out of the anesthesia, and I'd take care of the baby. I wanted to be involved."

While there is often an element of disappointment among those men who could not participate in a cesarean birth, there are some data[55] suggesting that fathers of children born by cesarean sections are exceptionally involved with their offspring in the early months. (Certainly a mother's need for help with the baby is greater for a woman recuperating from surgery than for a woman who has delivered vaginally, but other less practical factors may also be involved.)

MULTIPLE BIRTH

Generally couples know that they will be having twins (or more!), but not always. Whether they learn about a multiple birth at the time of delivery or before, their initial reaction is likely to reflect a mixture of overwhelming confusion, shock, and excitement. A multiple birth may hold greater risks for both the mother and the babies. Twins present enormous emotional, financial, and logistical problems—problems not shared by parents of single babies, problems that will be with the family for years to come. (Of course, twins also have a self-contained playgroup, which is generally an asset!)

The parents of twins may need more help than other new parents, especially in the beginning. A multiple birth forces mom and dad to become practical more quickly than parents who have only one baby. Of course, it is important that parents in this situation remember that their babies are individuals and should be treated as such from the very start. Still, it helps to realize that each baby does not need a bath every day, that naps can be organized, that two babies can nurse simultaneously, and so on.

If you and your partner suddenly discover that you are the parents of two or more new babies, try to find a group of parents who share your happy predicament. Such groups are very supportive and can offer a great deal of good advice to the frazzled couple.

WHEN TRAGEDY STRIKES

Birth of a Baby with a Congenital Disease

Certain physical handicaps, forms of mental retardation, or congenital dysfunctions (such as heart disease) can be detected at birth. When one of these problems occurs, the parents often experience overwhelming emotions—including shock, anger, sadness, denial, self-pity, shame, guilt, and envy directed toward parents of unaffected children. These feelings are to be expected since the parents must grieve over the loss of the baby they expected before they can begin to become attached to the baby that they have. It is especially important that parents maintain communication with each other through this difficult period of adjustment. As soon as possible, the parents should begin to search out those support systems (parent groups, agencies, and so on) available to help them. Such groups understand the special needs of children with specific problems, and their parents' needs as well. Often the group offers programs to assist parents in fostering their child's optimal development.

Stillbirth

The birth of a dead baby is always a tragedy. Sometimes a stillbirth is the result of a uterine infection or occurs because the umbilical cord is wrapped tightly around the fetus' neck. Sometimes there is no medical explanation.

As with the death of any loved one, the father and mother will mourn the loss of their baby, even if they have never held it or taken it home. It is crucial that parents share their feelings with one another during this time, for they may find that few of their friends or relatives understand the depth of their sadness. Grieving may continue for six to twelve months, and at times longer.

Even if the baby is stillborn, many parents find it helpful to see and touch their baby and to have a small memorial service. Although these are possibilities no one likes to consider, perhaps you and your partner should briefly discuss some of these options during pregnancy since it is not easy to make rational decisions following such a crisis.

We have seen that the complications associated with pregnancy, labor, and birth can range from those that are easy to weather to those that are truly tragic. Conscious or subconscious fears of these complications are familiar to all expectant parents. No one cares to dwell on the unpleasant, but many parents-to-be find that they are able to allay their fears somewhat by familiarizing themselves with these problems. Then, should the unexpected event occur in their own birth experience, they may be better equipped to deal with the consequences.

CHAPTER NINE

The Postpartum Period

The twenty-four hours following delivery are known as the immediate postpartum period. Your partner will be observed carefully during this time for signs of bleeding or infection. Usually you and your baby will be able to accompany her to the recovery room where she will stay for one to two hours until her vital signs (temperature, pulse, and blood pressure) have stabilized. She has been through a lot, and her body must adapt to the immediate weight loss of ten to fifteen pounds (the combined weight of the baby, placenta, blood, and other fluids). Periodically a nurse will check her vital signs, the amount of bloody vaginal discharge (called lochia) from her uterus, and the condition of her fundus. By feeling the fundus (the upper portion of the uterus), the nurse can tell whether or not the uterus is contracting properly as it returns to its prepregnant state. A soft uterus may be a sign of internal bleeding. The nurse may press down on the fundus frequently to stimulate its contractions.

In the recovery room, the two of you will finally be able to talk about your birth experience. Both of you may feel a mixture of elation and exhaustion. Naturally, you will reflect on the miracle of birth and the work that you both have accomplished. Treasure the moment.

Sometimes new parents find that they feel peculiar or disoriented. You may have trouble believing that this tiny baby is really yours. In the words of one father:

> *All of a sudden I realized we were parents. I was a father and Beth was a mother to this complete stranger. I wondered when I would begin to feel any love for this child. There were so many things to think about, all of a sudden, that Beth and I spent the moments talking hurriedly—almost incoherently—each bringing up something else that seemed important at the time.*

Some fathers feel somewhat left out of the picture, because they have received the least attention of all, even after having been such a marvelous support person through the birth. Don't be upset at yourself if you feel ambivalent. Ask how and what your partner is feeling; she may feel the way you do. Often a new mother is sore from the long period of exertion, or feels too tired to stay awake. She may want to tell you how much you did for her, or she may just want you to be near her. Another father told us:

I think I felt best when Gayle said, "Honey, you were great. I never could have done it without you. Even though it was rough going for a few hours, you gave me the strength to keep at it. And now look at how we are blessed. Just look at our new son."

If your partner is planning to breastfeed the baby, it will help her if she can start nursing when she is on the delivery table or in the recovery room. Your baby is likely to be more alert at that time than he or she will be in the next few hours. Some babies are born with a natural and strong sucking reflex. Others make only minimal, awkward first attempts at sucking. Your encouragement and support can make a tremendous difference in your partner's longterm success in nursing the baby.

About the time your partner is taken to her room, the baby is taken to the nursery for observation. If you can hold out this long, you will be able to call your relatives and friends together from her room. Both of you should enjoy the thrill of being together when you share your exciting news with the new grandparents and other close friends. An extra hour won't make much difference now. Spreading the news can be an exciting activity you do together as new parents.

THOSE FIRST DAYS IN THE HOSPITAL

The period immediately following the birth of your baby, up to the time when the baby and your partner leave the hospital for home, is likely to be a happy but somewhat unsettling period. Typically, you and your partner will experience moments of high energy, alternating with overwhelming fatigue.

Fathers may feel especially disoriented during this period. While the new mother stays at the hospital, becomes somewhat accustomed to hospital routine, and eagerly sets out to get to know her tiny child, the father must divide his time between two or three different worlds—hospital, home, and business.

You should not leave the hospital until both you and your partner feel comfortable about your departure. Whenever you do leave, make sure that your partner knows where you are going and when you plan to return. Find out if she needs anything that she may have forgotten to bring with her. Also, let the staff know where you will be in case they have to reach you for any reason.

When you first return home, you may find that your excitement is mixed with loneliness. (Loneliness is one emotion that a man participating in a home birth does not have to face.) Perhaps for the first time in many hours, you are alone. The quiet, calm atmosphere of your house or apartment can be quite a change after the activity and intensity of birth.

Of course, if you are not a first-time father, you might return home to the excited questions and unbridled enthusiasm of the new baby's brothers and sisters. No matter how tired you feel, you'll want to spend some time with them, relating the good news and giving them spoken and unspoken reassurances that their important positions in the household have not been usurped by a new addition. Perhaps your hospital has a sibling visitation policy, whereby brothers and sisters of the new baby are allowed to visit mother on the maternity unit and view the baby through the nursery window. Take advantage of this policy if it is available. That in-hospital reunion can be an important and meaningful event for the whole family.

Although you may want to be back at the hospital or start preparing for your family's return home, it is a good idea to slow down, eat something, take a shower, make a neighborhood birth announcement sign to hang in your window or on your tree, and then get some rest. (You will not have many opportunities for uninterrupted sleep in the months to come, so seize the chance!)

After a rest break, you may be busy running errands to prepare for the homecoming. You may have to buy supplies, set up the bassinet and changing table, arrange for diaper service, contact the pediatrician, buy food, and so on. Don't be overly concerned if you are not able to complete every task or locate every item on your shopping list. If everything is not perfect and in place, the baby will not object.

In many cases, new fathers have to put in some time at work—especially in those cases when the delivery preceded the due date. It's the wise and fortunate father who can arrange to take some "paternity leave" so he can get to know the baby at leisure and get some extra rest, too.

And, of course, you will want to be spending as much time as possible at the hospital enjoying the active and quiet moments with mother and child. Remember that some women are particularly sensitive in the first few days following the birth when they feel that the focus of attention has shifted so dramatically from them to the baby. One father we spoke to remembers his wife feeling very hurt when all her visitors went to the nursery window and spent most of the visiting hour looking at the babies. She needed attention at that time, too.

One of the most common aspects of family-centered care in hospitals is a rooming-in arrangement that allows the baby to stay with its mother in her room all day and night, except for public visiting hours or when the mother requests the baby be cared for in the nursery. This kind of set-up has distinct advantages: breastfeeding can succeed more easily if the baby is fed on demand, and new parents can profit from the advice of hospital staff members and gain confidence in their ability to handle the nitty-gritty elements of baby care. Generally you can remain in your partner's room to fully participate in baby care. With rooming-in, the father's status is not that of a visitor but that of the integral family member that he is.

You will find that there is a lot to learn about caring for an infant. Some hospitals cater to their "captive audience" and offer daily baby-care classes and discussion groups. These are often much appreciated by first-time parents. Some hospitals honor you and your partner by presenting you with a special steak-and-champagne dinner after the birth (charged to your hospital bill, of course!) Fathers are often welcome in the well-baby nursery to pick up or deliver their babies. In the intensive care nursery, there is often a twenty-four hour accessibility policy so that fathers can watch, photograph, or help care for a premature infant or a baby under close observation.

UNEXPECTED EVENTS DURING THE POSTPARTUM PERIOD

Postpartum Hemorrhage

This is a condition in which there is excessive bleeding after delivery, usually due to the retention of placental fragments which prevents the uterus from becoming firm. If your partner begins to hemorrhage, she will be watched very closely by nurses and doctors who will massage her uterus frequently to firm it up. (It will look as though they are massaging her stomach.) If the bleeding continues, the doctor may advise a D & C (dilation and curettage) operation to eliminate the fragments from the lining of the uterus. If the bleeding is due to the inability of the uterus to become firm for another reason (such as the delivery of a large baby or the experience of long labor), she will be given medication to stimulate uterine contraction. This medication is given either intravenously or intramuscularly.

Neonatal Jaundice

With neonatal jaundice, the baby's skin and the whites of the baby's eyes begin to take on a yellowish tinge. Red blood cells in the baby break down and release bilirubin, which the immature liver cannot remove from the circulation. The level of bilirubin is measured by analyzing a few drops of blood taken from the baby's heel. As the levels of bilirubin rise, the baby becomes more yellow and often more lethargic.

The first treatment for neonatal jaundice involves placing the baby under fluorescent lights, commonly known as "bili-lights." With the baby's eyes protected by gauze pads, he or she remains under the lights, except for feedings, for about twelve to eighteen hours a day. The lights help break down the bilirubin so it can be excreted. If the bilirubin levels still do not go down after a few days of phototherapy, the neonatologist may suspect that there is some kind of blood incompatibility between the mother's blood and the baby's blood. (The two most common types of blood imcompatibility are Rh and ABO.) If this is the case, the doctor may recommend an exchange transfusion in which the baby's bilirubin-laden blood is replaced with fresh whole blood.

Neonatal jaundice is usually easy to control, but in certain instances a baby may have to remain in the hospital for a few extra days after the mother is discharged. Sometimes the mother is readmitted to the hospital so she can continue to nurse her baby. To make the days pass quickly, visit the baby frequently and take comfort in knowing that the empty cradle at home will soon be filled by a healthy baby.

Postpartum Blues

It is important to realize that even though you and your partner are probably thrilled about the new baby, both of you may experience some "down" days anywhere from a fews days to a few weeks after the baby is born. Much of it can be traced to the adjustments that schedule changes and new demands are inflicting on both of you.

Many women experience an emotional letdown on the fourth to seventh day after delivery. This is often called the "blues" and is related to a combination of excitement and hormonal changes. Frequently, after birth, women are upset with their physical appearance. Your partner will find that her abdomen is still quite distended and that she has not lost all the weight she thought she would. She will feel tired, and she may feel overwhelmed by the responsibility a newborn imposes. She may be somewhat nervous about breastfeeding, waiting for her milk to come in, wondering if it will. She has received a great deal of admiring attention over the last several months, but now she may feel ignored as well-meaning friends and relatives shift their focus from her to the baby.

She will need to share her anxieties with the person closest to her—you. Encourage her, build up her confidence as a new mother, tell her she is doing a good job. She might benefit from some free time away from the baby and help in domestic affairs. Most of all, she will need to hear you say you love her.

The blues each of you may experience will subside more quickly if you can share them. Take time to communicate your needs and listen to each other in a nonjudgmental way. Remember, fatigue exacerbates depressed feelings. You and your partner should make sleep a top priority, napping whenever possible, or even hiring a babysitter to enable you to get some rest. It is amazing how much better the world looks when you are rested.

THE UPHEAVAL IN YOUR EMOTIONAL LIFE

How are you going to feel in your early days as a father? Many books are written about the feelings common to new mothers. Where does the new father fit into the picture?

You may be both fascinated and terrified by the baby. You will experience a wide range of unfamiliar feelings—some wonderful, some frightening—and be troubled by how little time you have to examine them. Because newborns need nourishment frequently, and cry to let you know it, you will be exhausted from round-the-clock interruptions in your sleep. Also, you might be taking over some of your partner's normal activities, and this will further crowd your daily schedule.

Your mother, mother-in-law, nurse, or other friend may come to help for a while. This may be a mixed blessing. However, if you must be away during those first few days after the birth, it is important that your partner have someone who can help her and be with her. Help of this kind is much appreciated, but the addition of a third adult in your home may cause some conflict. You may be told what to do and how to do it, and you may resent all the advice. After all, the baby is yours. One father said he felt like a nonperson as attention was showered on mother and baby. "Not once did my in-laws ask me what it was like for me to be at Teddy's birth," he said with chagrin. With outside help, expect some tension in the household and be prepared to put up with some of the negative feelings that may arise in you.

If local friends offer to help you, accept their offers. If they seem uncertain as to how they might help, they might welcome a suggestion from you. Perhaps they can prepare a meal or do some errands for you. One father told us he still remembers the wonderful aroma of an apple pie a neighbor baked in his kitchen the day after his wife came home from the hospital. "I couldn't believe that something so luscious had been produced in the midst of our chaos," he said.

ADJUSTMENTS IN SEXUAL INTIMACY

Most doctors and midwives tell their obstetrical patients to refrain from intercourse until they have been seen for a postpartum office visit. Often abstinence is not a problem for couples busy with a new baby, extra housework, and visitors. For some, however, it becomes another area of stress. You should refrain from intercourse long enough to allow the uterus and episiotomy to heal properly and to limit the possibility of postpartum infection. The uterus is considered healed when the lochia (bloody vaginal discharge) subsides, usually two-and-a-half to three weeks after delivery. The stitches taken to close the episiotomy begin to feel better within a week.

In the meantime you can certainly engage in those forms of lovemaking that do not involve penetration of the vagina. A woman may experience orgasm during this time without hurting her uterus or her stitches. In fact, after pregnancy, a woman often finds she experiences heightened feelings of orgasm because of the changes her body has undergone.

In resuming sexual intercourse, you are likely to find some things are different from before. Your partner may find intercourse uncomfortable for some time after childbirth. This may be due to the healing of the episiotomy. It may help if you shift your position a bit. Because of hormonal changes (estrogen deprivation), a woman will not produce adequate lubrication during sexual activity, and this, too, can cause discomfort during intercourse. The woman who is breastfeeding may experience this decreased lubrication longer than the woman who is not nursing. To prevent discomfort and the strain that it involves, use saliva, lubricated jelly (such as K-Y Jelly), or a contraceptive cream during foreplay. (If you are using condoms or a diaphragm, avoid petroleum jelly—Vaseline—since it can cause deterioration of the rubber or latex.)

Women who have given birth by cesarean delivery may be fearful about disrupting their scar and often find it painful to have the man lie on top of them. If this is true in your partner's case, use positions that do not involve putting your weight on her abdomen.

Your partner may not menstruate for some months after the baby is born. However, it is important to use some form of contraception whenever you engage in sexual intercourse because you cannot be sure when she will resume ovulation. Breastfeeding is not a reliable method of birth control. If your partner is breastfeeding, she should *not* use birth control pills. They can diminish her milk supply and cause high concentrations of hormones in her milk; the hormones can be passed on to the nursing infant. If your partner used a diaphragm before her pregnancy, she should be refitted for a new one since her size may have changed. Many couples use a combination of condoms and contraceptive foam until they make further decisions about birth control.

For some couples the question is not what kind of birth control to use, or what position is most comfortable, but rather, "Will we ever have sex again?" Some men report a marked reduction in sexual desire, which many believe is due to their perpetual fatigue and their awareness that baby is nearby. Some men we spoke to mentioned other causes. One father felt his disinterest in sex was directly related to his close participation in his child's birth. He explained that the experience had been so emotionally overwhelming that he felt drained of the drive and energy he associated with sexual activity. Another father suggested it had something to do with a lingering taboo regarding a woman who has just given birth. (The issue of the woman as both sacred and cursed is discussed in Chapter Four.)

There was also some suggestion that the woman's body, for a time, belonged to the newborn. This theme seemed particularly strong in cases where the mother was breastfeeding. During orgasm or at moments of sexual excitement, a woman who is breastfeeding may find that milk leaks from her breasts. Fathers sometimes experience some confusion about their partner's breasts and their dual role as sources of milk for the baby and sources of sexual pleasure.

> *Postpartum, the lactating breasts may be perceived differently by both wife and husband. Some men are repelled by the increased size, the milk, and the dripping; others are aroused. Other couples say that when the woman is lactating, they don't want to involve the breasts in sex; they feel the breasts are only for the baby and should be confined to the nurturing role.*[56]

You may notice that your disinterest in sex is matched by your partner's. A woman's reduced desire may be attributed to a number of factors: increased fatigue, tender breasts, worry about stitches, hormonal readjustment, concern about her appearance, anticipation of pain during intercourse, worry about the baby's awakening, and/or fear of initiating a new pregnancy. These factors may also affect your partner's ability to experience orgasm.

While sexual activity is reduced for many couples, these couples often report a heightened sense of affection and closeness with each other. Some fathers felt that getting a babysitter and going out for a romantic before-baby style dinner did wonders for their relationship with their partner. "Corny as it sounds," one father said, "after the baby's birth, Sarah and I really needed the romance to get into the mood." Another father told us about his experience:

> *We were too tired to go out. We needed someone to take the baby out. The times we really missed were our old Saturday afternoons. Before Brett, we used to get work done around the house, take a shower, take a late nap, and then get up for a late dinner out. In those first hectic months after the baby, our nicest "dates" were when my sister took Brett for a couple of hours so that we could settle in at home. Instead of eating dinner out, we'd pick up a pizza when we'd pick up Brett. But those couple of hours alone were just what we needed.*

The easiest situation, of course, is when both of you have similar sexual needs. If you are both interested in resuming regular sexual activity, you may need to make certain adjustments. While the physiological changes fall to your partner, both of you may face emotional adjustments that will affect your sexual relations. You will both be tired from the new experience of parenthood, and this can create sexual tension for one or both of you. In the adjustment period after the birth of your child, share and communicate love in as many ways as you can. The following advice is from couples who have been through it:

- Talk to each other about what's happening.
- Spend quiet time together, even though it may require much planning.
- Understand that this period is temporary; your sex life will improve.
- Be affectionate with each other.
- Be affectionate with your new infant.
- Try to maintain a sense of humor.

FEELING LIKE A FAMILY

In the postpartum period, you and your partner will have to strive for effective communication to reduce some of the inevitable difficulties in adjusting to life with a new baby. While you may be particularly aware of changes in your sex life, there may be other alterations that will also affect your relationship with your partner. There may be times when you will long for "the good ol' days" when you and your partner were free to share conversation, evening meals, and sexual pleasure without interruption. Dr. Lucy Waletsky, a psychiatrist at Georgetown University Hospital, feels that the postpartum period can be less stressful if couples are realistic about the adjustments that parenthood can bring.

> *Expectations must be changed so that, instead of an idealized picture of postpartum happiness, couples expect stress to accompany parenthood. . . . Thus forewarned, couples can include humor and patience in their overall approach to the emotional difficulties that arise. This attitude is possible when it is*

> *understood that such turbulence need not be hidden or denied, but can serve as a stimulus for growth in the relationship.*[57]

The postpartum time can actually be a creative period during which you undergo an important transition. At the end of this period, you will probably have learned much about your partner, your baby, and yourself. You will no longer be a couple with a baby; you will be a family.

CHAPTER TEN

Life with Baby

Certain people who are unfamiliar with babies—even expectant mothers and fathers—sometimes say that a newborn isn't a very engaging creature, just a funny little human being who sleeps, cries, feeds, and eliminates. Some expectant parents wonder how they're ever going to relate to a person with such a limited repertoire. If you haven't had much opportunity to be around infants, you may think they don't really become alert, responsive, and interesting until they sit up, crawl, walk, or even talk. If your expectations are along these lines, prepare yourself for a pleasant surprise.

WHAT YOUR BABY CAN DO

Your baby, even at birth, is an incredibly competent, well-organized human being. He can already begin, sustain, and end social exchanges. He can see, smell, hear, and taste. If your partner was not medicated during labor and delivery, your baby may be extremely alert in the first hour after birth. Later he is likely to sink into a deep sleep lasting several hours.[58] This deep sleep helps babies recover from the exhausting birth process and gives them time to adjust to the new demands of extrauterine life. Sometimes babies sleep so soundly on the second or third day, it seems almost impossible to wake them up.

Your baby can see as soon as he is born. If you jiggle an object about twelve to fifteen inches in front of his eyes, he may focus on it. Once he focuses, move the object slowly to one side. He may follow it briefly with his eyes or even with his eyes and head. Babies prefer to look at an animated human face. They will follow a face-like oval for 180 degrees, but they will follow a picture of a "scrambled" face (one with the eyes and mouth in the wrong positions) only a fraction of that distance.[59] Interestingly, twelve to fifteen inches is approximately the distance from a baby's eyes to his parent's face while he is being held for feedings.

Your baby will be very responsive to sound at birth and may have been responsive even before birth. Researchers have shown that the fetus will startle when loud sounds are made close to the abdomen of his mother. A woman violinist observed that during her pregnancy her baby became very agitated whenever she played Wagner. You may notice that immediately after birth, your baby will turn his head to the human voice, especially to the higher pitch of the female voice or when you raise the pitch of your voice.[60]

Infants also can recognize the difference between human and nonhuman sounds, and they demonstrate this by using different sucking patterns in response to each.[61] As early as the second day of life, infants will move in rhythm to human speech, but not to disconnected syllables.[62] When researchers did frame-by-frame analyses of films of newborns listening to people talking, they found that the almost imperceptible movements the babies made (such as extending fingers or turning their heads slightly) were coordinated in time with the intonation and pauses of the speaker. This "entrainment" has been described as a dance between the newborn and parent.[63]

Your newborn will also have well-developed senses of smell and taste. Babies show their preference for the aroma of milk over the smell of water or sugar water by turning their heads to milk.[64] By the fifth day of life, breastfed infants can discriminate between their own mother's breast pads and those of other women.[65] Infants can also discriminate between human milk in a bottle and cow's milk formula in a bottle; they use a different sucking pattern for each.[66]

Many of these amazing abilities of the newborn were not recognized or appreciated until recently, because babies only show these complex visual and auditory capacities when they are in a quiet, alert state. A fussy, hungry baby will be too overwhelmed by hunger to display these responses. In the last twenty years, researchers have recognized that babies move through several "states of consciousness" in the course of each day, or even within each hour.[67,68] What used to seem like a "buzzing blooming confusion" of behavior now is seen as an orderly progression of states—from deep or active sleep, through active or quiet wakefulness, to fussiness and hard crying. Babies often work to maintain the state they are in. For example, sleeping babies must shut out distracting noises and sights in order to remain asleep. Likewise, to look at something, babies must inhibit the jerky movements their uncoordinated bodies produce spontaneously. Newborns are already amazingly able "to keep themselves under control" through various devices. Sucking fingers or thumbs is one of the best ways infants have of soothing themselves and maintaining a particular state.

Although your newborn is capable of maintaining a steady state, his immaturity and lack of coordination often upset the balance. Early on, for example, you may notice that he always has bowel movements when he is asleep and that these bowel movements always wake him. As time passes, his internal systems will become coordinated so that bowel movements will come closer to feedings and sleep will be free for rest. Studies have shown that regular interventions by the caregiver—feeding the hungry baby, rocking the fussy one—help the infant synchronize his body's functions.[69]

FEEDING YOUR BABY

During pregnancy, you and your partner will undoubtedly discuss whether you would like your baby to be breastfed or bottlefed. In many ways parents' and baby's routines will be affected by this choice. Breastfed babies are likely to be hungry every two or three hours, whereas bottlefed babies may go four hours between feedings. This is because human breast milk is more digestible than formula, so the baby's stomach empties more quickly with breast milk.

Your decision will also determine who will feed the baby. If your baby is bottlefed, you can begin giving her some of her feedings from the start. If your child is breastfed, however, it is important that the new mother build up a good, stable milk supply. Since her supply is determined by demand, it is best (barring any medical reasons for supplementation) that the baby solely nurse for the first six to eight weeks. The baby's vigorous, frequent sucking will cause your partner's milk to come in and increase to an amount that will satisfy the baby's hunger.

No matter what feeding method you select, remember there is always a role that the father can play. If your child is bottlefed, your partner may need your assistance in buying and preparing formula, and in sterilizing and preparing bottles. If your baby is breastfed, the new mother will need your emotional support in order to feel comfortable and relaxed enough to nurse successfully. In addition, once your partner's milk supply has been established, she can express milk into a bottle for you to give to your baby.

Your baby should be fed when she is hungry and awake. If you are giving her a bottle, find a place where you can be comfortable and relaxed as you nestle her in your arms. The baby will swallow most easily if she's held in a semisitting position. It may help to place some pillows under your arm. Hold the bottle so that milk, not air, fills the nipple.

Do not be tempted to prop the bottle, even with a safe holder. Feeding involves much more than getting food into the baby. The warmth, smell, and close contact that come with being held lovingly are as important to your baby's development as good nutrition. Furthermore, babies whose bottles are propped are more likely to develop ear infections. When your baby is older, do not give her a bottle to take to bed. Babies who fall asleep with bottles in bed are more likely to develop cavities (from the pool of milk that soaks their teeth).

Once or twice during each feeding, try to burp your baby by holding her up against your shoulder or placing her, tummy down, across your knees. Gently pat or rub her back to help expel the air she has swallowed.

Depending on your baby's size and how vigorously she sucks, a feeding may last from five to twenty-five minutes. Never push a baby to finish the entire contents of a bottle. Let her appetite be your guide. Like adults, babies' appetites will vary from meal to meal. Sometimes she'll drink a lot and not be hungry again for hours. Other times she may fall asleep in the middle of a feeding, only to waken after a short time and need to be fed again. This unpredictability will probably be greatest in the first month of life when babies are relatively disorganized creatures.

Healthy bottlefed infants may want six to nine bottles per day. Because of the nature of human milk, a breast fed baby probably will need even more. By the end of the first month, most bottlefed babies will have developed their own fairly regular schedules.

If your partner has decided to breastfeed the baby, consider yourself a fortunate father. Your baby will be getting human milk—a rich, easily digestible, nutritious, natural food, the perfect food for the human infant. Your partner will benefit as well, because nursing relieves her of the chore of making formula and washing bottles. She will be able to rest during nursing and store up her energy for other activities. In addition, you will save money, you will never have to get up to prepare midnight feedings, and you will have a child with fewer allergies and illnesses.

The early breast milk is called colostrum. Your infant receives this in the first two to five days of nursing. Colostrum, or early milk, is a clear yellowish fluid that provides exactly the right balance of nutrients needed by a newborn. It is high in several proteins (including enzymes and antibodies) which can protect your baby from infection. When the nursing mother's body is fighting off infection, the antibodies she produces are passed through her milk to the baby, so the breastfed infant has fewer respiratory and gastrointestinal infections. In families with a history of allergies, breast milk becomes even more important, for breastfed babies develop fewer and/or less severe allergies than bottlefed babies.[70]

The milk your partner produces is nutritionally superior to any cow's milk or soy-based formula and is specifically suited to the metabolism of your newborn. Breast milk is high in cholesterol, which is necessary for the developing infant and which may make cholesterol less of a threat in adult years. (It seems that the body's ability to handle cholesterol may be acquired very early in life. Adults who were breastfed as babies show lower cholesterol levels than those who were bottlefed.) The composition of breast milk changes over time to adjust to the changing needs of the child.[71] Because human milk is so nutritious and substantial, your growing infant will be well-nourished for six months to one year without needing to eat high-calorie solid foods.

The breastfed baby is less likely to become obese during infancy, childhood, or adulthood. This is probably due, in part, to the fact that your baby determines how much milk she will take at each feeding. You or your partner will not be able to insist that a bottle be emptied before a feeding is over.

As natural as breastfeeding may seem to an experienced mother, initially a new mother may find it difficult and frustrating. One reason for this is that mothers are often encouraged to "token" breastfeed.

> *Token breastfeeding is characterized by severe limitation of social customs from the day of birth to the day of eventual total weaning. . . . There are rules restricting the number of feedings, the duration of feedings, the amount of time between feedings, and the amount of mother-baby contact that stimulates the urge to suck.*[72]

It is unfortunate that advice about breastfeeding is often based on guidelines appropriate for bottlefeeding. Such advice can, in fact, interfere with the breastfeeding relationship. Bottlefeeding mothers may be encouraged to feed their babies by the clock, usually once every four hours. But this policy makes little sense for the nursing mother and child, since human milk is low in fat and protein, and the amount the mother produces depends on sucking stimulation from the baby. In fact, human milk most resembles the milk of other animal species in which there is almost constant mother-infant contact and essentially continuous feeding.[73] Thus, as your baby grows, the only way your partner will produce the proper amount of milk is if your baby nurses more frequently. Nursing, therefore, cannot work on a strict four-hour schedule. Although nursing seems to be continuous at first, with time the baby will nurse less frequently and more rapidly.

The mother who nurses her baby frequently is likely to hear upsetting remarks like, "You just fed her an hour ago." Unless she knows the facts about breast milk, she may begin to wonder if she is producing enough milk, if her milk is good, or if she is spoiling her baby by feeding her every time she indicates hunger.

This is where you can have a direct and crucial impact on your partner's success in breastfeeding. When your partner worries because the baby cries to eat every two hours, remind her that babies digest breast milk quickly. This can allay her fear that her milk supply is inadequate. When your mother voices her doubts that the baby can gain weight on breast milk alone, express your confidence that she will. When your partner complains that breastfeeding leaves her no time to get work done, reassure her that nursing is the top priority for a new mother.

If you are not already predisposed to nursing, you may feel more positive about it and be able to give your partner better support if your read one of the books about breastfeeding listed in the bibliography (see page 259). You will discover that milk production is an amazing process. Even though all women are physically capable of nursing, some find it difficult to breastfeed satisfactorily. It is important that your partner be relaxed in the first, often trying, weeks of lactation. Once she and the baby become adjusted to one another (sometimes only after a few weeks of trial and error), nursing can be a breeze. Your emotional support is crucial in getting them over the hump. In fact, one study has shown that the most important factor in breastfeeding success is the presence of a support person to "mother the mother."[74] The woman who receives support from her partner is, quite simply, more successful at breastfeeding.

Though you may fully understand the value of breast milk for your baby and can identify with the baby's pleasure in such a warm and close relationship, you may still feel somewhat uneasy about your partner's decision to breastfeed. For one thing, your partner may place more demands on you because a nursing mother requires more rest and encouragement than the mother who is bottlefeeding.[75] In addition, you may discover that you feel uncomfortable about what other people think, about who observes the feedings, and about how old your child will be when weaning occurs.

You may also have some lingering questions about whether your lack of involvement in feeding will somehow interfere with your baby's attachment to you.

Some fathers feel left out when their partners breastfeed. Because mother and child are engrossed in each other so much of the time, jealous feelings sometimes crop up. A new father may not have much uninterrupted time with his partner. In addition, he may feel that he cannot compete with her for the baby's love or attention. A father who feels this way may also feel that his partner is more concerned with the baby than she is with him. Your baby may need its mother at certain times when you, too, need her. It is admittedly difficult to adjust to the fact that you are often going to be the one who must wait. (Actually, this situation would hold true whether or not your partner is nursing, so long as she is the baby's main caretaker.)

Don't feel that nursing limits your parenting contribution. Some important studies in the past twenty years show that feeding is by no means the only root of love, that mealtime is not the only time when bonding takes place. Our growing awareness of the newborn's capacities suggests that all the baby's behaviors come into play as she develops bonds to other individuals. By means of seeing, hearing, sucking, smiling, clinging, and crying, a baby reaches out to her world. Those few people who consistently respond to these social overtures are the ones she grows to love.

Current research supports this contention. One provocative study with monkeys suggests that feeding alone is relatively unimportant in the development of a secure bond.

Infant monkeys were taken away from their natural mothers and raised in cages with two models of monkeys—one made of wire with a bottle attached, and one without a bottle but covered with cloth. Aside from eating, the infant monkeys spent most of their time on the cloth model. Whenever they became upset or frightened, they immediately ran to their cloth mother. The researchers concluded that the contact comfort was far more important than food in the development of an affectionate bond.[76]

Another study shows that regardless of the feeding method, fathers are much more involved with their newborns than our cultural stereotypes suggest. Fathers, mothers, and infants were observed together in the hospital two to four days after birth. Fathers tended to touch, hold, and talk to their babies more than mothers did, even though over half the babies were breastfed. Mothers, on the other hand, smiled at their babies more.[77]

In short, whether your baby is breastfed or bottlefed, you can give her love in many ways. Take time to talk to your baby, tell her about your day, hold her close, let her learn your touch, cuddle her so she learns what you smell like, respond when she cries, bathe her and change her. The more you relate to your child at an early age, the sooner she will get to know you and love you.

COMFORTING YOUR BABY

Even though your baby is surprisingly competent at birth, he is still utterly dependent on you and your partner and will be for many months to come. Compared to other species, the human newborn's motor abilities are very immature. This means that without the help of another person, your baby cannot snuggle up for warmth, move around to find food, or protect himself from danger. He can't even hold onto you as you move around. Without your active ministrations, your baby is lost.

But, as every new parent quickly learns, an infant does have some control over the care he receives. In addition to his wonderful abilities to respond to sights, sounds, and smells, he is born with a powerful means of initiating interactions with you. Your baby can cry. A baby's cry is so distressing, even painful, for us to hear that our immediate response is to try to stop it. By crying, your baby can call you to him when he feels uncomfortable. He can signal his need for help. You have the job of figuring out what is wrong.

Your baby cries for several reasons. He may be hungry, wet, tired, sick, in pain, or lonely. Sometimes you can tell what is bothering him immediately: a cold bare bottom may be uncomfortable during a diaper change or he may be very hungry after a long nap. At other times, the reason for his distress may not be clear, and you will have to try different ways to soothe him.

Sometimes you can help your baby by wrapping him securely in a blanket; this will make him feel snug and comfortable. You might try holding him securely so his arms and legs are not flailing. Some babies are soothed when they are patted gently on the back in a steady rhythm. Babies also like to be rocked and walked. One of the best ways to quiet a fussy baby is to bring him to your shoulder. Such movement through space, called vestibular stimulation, often helps the baby come to an alert state.[78] Some people call this the doll's eye response since the baby's eyes often open as he is brought to an upright position.

If you come to your baby soon after he begins crying, it will take you less time to help him calm down. If you wait until he is really screaming, it may take you much longer to quiet him.

Regardless of how uncertain you feel about your ability to interpret your infant's cries, you communicate an important message by coming to him at these times. You are helping him develop a basic trust in you and in the world you represent. Dr. Lee Salk, a psychologist, has written, "There is no harm in a child crying; the harm is done if his cries are not answered."[79]

This point of view contrasts with the widespread notion that newborns need to cry and will be spoiled if parents don't allow them to cry. Some studies suggest that this is simply not true. Babies do not cry to exercise their lungs. Before the infant first breathes, the lungs are deflated. But within one-third of a second after breathing begins, the lungs become expanded and remain expanded from then on.[80]

Responding to your crying baby does not mean you are spoiling him. One study has shown that the more promptly and consistently parents responded to a baby's cries, the less—in frequency and duration—the baby cried at one year of age. In addition, babies whose cries were answered appeared more independent at one year and had developed other means, beyond crying, to express their needs or wishes.[81]

In the last few years, it has become popular for parents to carry their young infants close to their bodies in front carriers made of soft cloth. The baby is thereby close to the adult's chest and can feel the rhythm of the parent's heartbeat. The warmth and movement are likely to be soothing to your baby and pleasureable to you, too. Some of the carriers are designed to support the infant who cannot yet hold up his head. This allows you to have your hands free so you can be close to your baby and calm him while you engage in other activities.

Based on their belief that a newborn needs closeness and warmth even at night, a growing number of couples are bringing their babies to bed with them. While there are many (including Dr. Spock) who caution against such a practice, parents are making their own decisions. Getting the baby out of the pattern of sleeping with mom and dad at some later date does not seem to pose any unusual problems.[82]

Whenever your newborn cries he is expressing a legitimate need. That is not to say you can never let him cry. Sometimes, at the end of a hectic day, he will be overtired or overly excited, and you may find that the usual comforting measures do not help. In fact, your repeated attempts to soothe him may just upset him more. He may manage best if left alone to cry off his tension.

Some babies actually may need to fuss a little before settling down to sleep. Others will work themselves into a frenzy if left to cry. Getting to know your baby and learning how to comfort his distress may be one of the more trying aspects of fathering. But it will get easier with practice, and, as your baby gets older, he will learn to soothe himself some of the time.

PLAYING WITH YOUR BABY

Play has been called the work of children. Through play children explore the physical and social characteristics of their world, practice new skills, try on new roles, and enjoy their sensory and motor abilities. Although your newborn will not play with gleeful abandon until she is somewhat older, she will enjoy social interactions with you from early on.

Your baby is born with an urge toward mastery. Beginning in the first days, you will see her working to perfect her visual and auditory skills. She will watch and follow your face when it captures her attention. She will also turn to a sound to locate its source. She may smile, not as the result of a gas pain, but in pleasure at being gently stroked or at hearing soft sounds that appeal to her. Within a short time, she will begin to practice holding her head erect when you hold her at your shoulder or while she is lying on her stomach. Within weeks she will begin making the jerky swipes at the air that eventually will be perfected into coordinated reaching. By playing with your newborn, you will be providing encouragement and opportunities for her to explore and expand these capabilities.

In our culture, both parent and infant seem to enjoy playful face-to-face interactions. By the time your infant is three weeks old, she will have learned to discriminate between her mother, you, and a stranger, and she will expect different kinds of "play" with each of you. It has been found that in parent-infant interaction, fathers present "a more playful, jazzing up approach." Dr. Brazelton has written,

> *As one watches this interaction, it seems that a father is expecting a more heightened playful response from the baby. And he gets it! Amazingly enough, an infant by 2 or 3 weeks displays an entirely different attitude (more wide-eyed, playful and bright-faced) toward his father than to his mother.*[83]

One mother commented that she was amazed at her partner's play sessions with their six-week-old baby. The new father spent over an hour each evening cooing, making faces, sticking out his tongue, and nibbling their baby's ears and nose. Whenever the father approached, the baby became excited. One evening the father offered a first bottle to this breastfed baby. His daughter licked the nipple, sucked, and got some milk. Suddenly she gave him a look of wide-eyed surprise. She seemed to be shocked that milk was coming from her favorite playmate.

In addition to these two types of play—that of providing opportunities for your baby to master her environment and engaging in lively face-to-face exchanges—you can start another important kind of social interaction during your baby's first weeks. You can begin to sing and read to her. Certain songs and books are wonderfully soothing to infants because of their repetitive rhythms. Long before your baby understands the words, she will respond to the cadence of the verse. Stories like *Goodnight Moon*[84] and *The Runaway Bunny*[85] are wonderful beginning books because of their simplicity and rhythmic quality: "Goodnight moon. Goodnight cow jumping over the moon. Goodnight light and the red balloon. . . ." As you read these stories over and over, their very familiarity becomes pleasurable and comforting to your child. You will be amazed that as soon as she begins to speak, she will be able to repeat many of the key words. And you will see her sheer delight, her feelings of competence, as she begins to master this new world of language.

Chapter Eleven will explain a wide variety of physical exercises you can do with your baby. These activities, which you will both enjoy, can become an important part of your daily play together.

CHAPTER ELEVEN

Interaction and Exercise

Written by Jan Shaffer, Ph.D.

Once your baby has arrived, you will want to assist in her emotional and physical development. This chapter details how you can give your baby a head start toward emotional security and physical competence by engaging her in activities that both of you enjoy. The basic approach involves certain physical exercises that you can help your baby perform, accompanied by certain communicative techniques that you can employ anytime (but especially during the exercises) to enhance your baby's sense of well-being.

A baby develops mainly by interacting with himself, with his parents, and with inanimate objects that are presented to him. Even a brand new infant is ready to begin exercising. Chapter Ten discussed how recent research has shown that newborns are highly sensitive to, responsive to, and aware of their world. Futhermore, they are greatly influenced by their early experiences.

Newborns are essentially emotional creatures who communicate primarily on an emotional level. Crying is one of a baby's most powerful forms of communication. But crying is not merely a response to obvious discomforts like pain or hunger. Babies also cry for "unknown causes," although this pattern decreases sharply when a baby gets increased attention in the form of parental handling, talking, and looking.

Immediately after birth an infant's eyes begin to focus, and almost simultaneously she can discriminate shapes and patterns and track a slowly moving object. Newborns prefer to look at human faces, especially at the eyes. They respond to emotions communicated by the eyes and by facial expressions, and they show sensitivity to the emotional states of others, particularly parents. For this reason, it is never too soon to start communicating love to your child. Eye communication—coupled with pleasant words, smiles, and physical contact—will produce feelings of satisfaction, well-being, and self-esteem in your child. These feelings, in turn, will be the basis for her developing love toward you.

Eye contact and physical contact should be warm and spontaneous and should not be reserved as a reward given when your child does something to please you. Your child will learn the art of loving from you, so tender touches and eye contact are among the most precious gifts you can give her.

Besides the immediate and short-term rewards of interaction, early and deliberate involvement has spectacular longterm benefits. Babies who are handled, played with, smiled at, and talked to (and who are provided with objects to see, hear, and touch) are not only more attentive and coordinated as infants, but they retain these advantages in later life. Further, the amount and quality of stimulation provided to an infant are related to future scholastic performance. The data suggest that children who have more interaction and encouragement make rapid and enduring gains in mental development. Finally, the more varied the stimulation presented to the baby, the more easily she will be able to adjust to new sights, sounds, movements, and feelings. For example, frequent parent-infant eye contact will instill in an infant the capacity and self-confidence to initiate and maintain eye contact later on. Although eye contact may seem to be an elementary skill, it is one that frequently eludes emotionally deprived children. Its absence is often noted by preschool teachers as a characteristic related to anxiety and immaturity.

One particular form of interaction, physical exercise, offers many advantages to infants. While providing you with a perfect opportunity to engage in both eye contact and physical contact with your child, it promotes the development of motor skills, balance, coordination, and spatial orientation. It strengthens muscles to assure good posture and prevent skeletal deformities, and it imbues the child with self-confidence and alertness. Physical exercise is also an excellent way of dissipating stress, which infants sometimes experience as a result of noise, confusion, temperature changes, and immobility. Finally, exercise is a particularly fruitful way for a father to interact with his child. By showing himself to be stimulating, fun-loving, and attentive, the father sets the stage for a good parent-child relationship later on. It has even been suggested that an active father promotes his child's independence by drawing the baby out of the mother-infant nexus. Many species of animals prepare their offspring for independence and maturity through play, and in this regard, humans are no different.

Sometimes, however, fears of making a mistake and disturbing or hurting the baby deter parents from attempting infant exercise. Or a protective mother or in-law may discourage a father's more active play. The muscular relaxation that often characterizes a "quiet" baby can also be a deterrent. If you have misgivings of this sort, you should remember that infants are ingeniously designed to be sturdier than they appear. The benefits of exercising with your baby far outweigh any possible risks, as long as you use good judgment and do not overdo it. Exercising together can provide your child with the experience of feeling that she is special, one of a kind.

BEFORE YOU BEGIN

Before describing exercises for you and your baby to try, some general instructions are in order. Above all, remember to make the experience safe and fun. The instructions tell you how to perform the exercises safely. Your job is to provide the fun. You are your child's coach, trainer, and manager, and the benefits of the program depend mainly on your enthusiasm and effort.

How Old?

You can begin to do the following exercises with your baby when she is just a few days old. At first do just one or two exercises at a time, gradually increasing the number you do each day. Your first session should be limited to four or five minutes of activity. By the time the baby is a month old, you may have worked up to ten or fifteen minutes, depending on your baby's reactions. Use your baby's reactions as your gauge: stop the activity if she fusses or seems to turn away. Newborns can be overstimulated very easily. Proceed slowly, and be sure to support your baby's head if she cannot do so by herself.

When?

As you get to know your baby, you will see that she has fairly regular periods when she is especially alert and sociable. Save your exercises for one of these periods, rather than attempting activity when she is distracted by hunger or fatigue. Since babies enjoy routines, it is a good idea to link the exercise period to some other regular activity that your baby enjoys (bathing or changing diapers, for example).

Where?

Choose a safe location where you are comfortable and have room to move. The specific location is not of great consequence, but you should use the same location every day. Either a bed or the floor works well. The floor may be preferable, partly for reasons of safety and partly because having you on the floor gives your baby a chance to interact with you on her level. Since children spend most of their time looking up at adults, they especially enjoy those times when you are down on the floor with them.

How?

Remember to relax and maintain eye contact. Your baby will respond to the tone of your voice and the firmness of your hand. Be patient and do not try to force him along faster than his age and temperament allow. If he appears tense at first, gently massage his muscles to relax him. Avoid sudden or jerky movements. Observe your baby's reactions closely, sharing his pleasures, but also realizing that his attention span is very limited. Be careful not to prolong either a particular exercise or an exercise session, especially at first. Since babies enjoy repetition and consistency, do the same basic program in the same place every day, introducing only one change at a time.

Music and singing are useful accompaniments to exercising. If you expose your child to rhythm early, he will later find it easy to learn to dance, sing, or play an instrument. Developing a sense of rhythm also contributes to stamina, since people without bodily rhythm tire more easily because their muscles fight one another. As an added bonus, singing encourages speech development.

Remember, too much stimulation can cause crying and irritability. You will soon learn which exercises your baby enjoys most and how many she can manage at a time. Sometimes the same exercise will excite a baby one day and quiet her the next. Don't be discouraged by such inconsistency. With babies, inconsistent behavior is the rule.

Equipment

The few items you may need for the following exercises can easily be found around the house: a toy, a dowel, a broomstick, and an ironing board.

Some Final Pointers

Make exercise time short. Try to quit before either of you gets too tired. Understand each exercise before you attempt to do it. Relax. Be patient. Do the exercises when your child is alert, but not right after eating. Give lots of hugs and kisses. And most of all, have fun.

1. ARM SWING

Why—Workout for the upper body, chest, and upper back. Helps prevent round shoulders.

How—Place your child on her back. Place your thumb in the center of your baby's hand and wrap her fingers around your finger. (This teaches her to grip, which she'll soon learn to do by herself.) First stretch her arms out to her sides, then cross them over her chest. Repeat, using a slow rhythm. Describe the movement in words to your baby so she will begin to identify the words with the action. For example, say "Open arms and close arms." If she becomes tense, don't force the movement. Massage her shoulder muscles to relax her arm. Try to maintain eye contact.

2. LEG PUSHES

Why—Strengthens stomach and leg muscles. Works the diaphragm and encourages deeper breathing.

How—Place your baby on his back. Hold his lower legs and bend his knees gently onto his tummy, thus causing his abdomen to pull in. Wait until the child exhales, then extend his legs straight along the floor. Do not press the abdomen for more than a few seconds on any given movement.

3. FLUCTUATING LEG PUSHES

Why—Strengthens stomach and leg muscles and stimulates muscle coordination.

How—Place your baby on his back. Hold his lower legs, and bend one knee gently onto his tummy while keeping his other leg straight. Now reverse the leg movements in a smooth and rhythmic pattern.

4. LEG STRETCH

Why—Strengthens lower back and leg and stomach muscles. Prepares the baby for the voluntary movement of turning over.

How—Place your baby on her back. With one hand, hold her right leg and gently stretch it out along the floor. With your other hand, hold your baby's left knee in a slightly bent position. Cross the left leg over the right and set the foot on the floor. The left hip and buttock will rise, rolling your baby toward the right side. Alternate legs, working up to three or four repetitions for each side.

5. ARM STRETCHES

Why—Strengthens the arms and upper back and the pectoral muscles.

How—Place your child on her back. Wrap her fingers around your thumbs. Use the same grip as in the Arm Swing exercise. Stretch her arms up over her head and lower them to the floor above her head with palms facing up. Now raise both arms up and then lower them to the floor at her sides with her palms facing down. Repeat, working up to several times. If your baby's arm muscles are tense, massage her shoulders until her arms relax and then proceed.

6. ALTERNATING ARM STRETCHES

Why—Helps muscle coordination and rhythm.

How—Place your baby on his back. Use the same thumb grip as in the Arm Stretch exercise. Place one arm on the floor above your child's head and the other arm on the floor by his side. Then simultaneously move each arm into the opposite position. Repeat several times.

7. LEG CIRCLES AND THE SCISSORS

Why—Stretches legs, waist, and inner thighs.

How—Place your baby on his back. With each of your hands, hold one of his lower legs. Then bend the legs at the knee and move them in a bicycle or circular motion. Repeat by moving his legs in the opposite direction. Shake his legs gently to release and relax the muscles. While your baby is still on his back, stretch both legs apart and lift them off the floor. Then open and close his legs in a scissors motion.

While your baby is lying flat on the bed or floor, try holding a toy above his legs. Bring his attention to the toy and encourage him to reach for it with his feet. If he reaches with his hands, hold them down gently to further encourage the use of his feet. Move the toy higher to increase the difficulty.

8. ROCK AND ROLL

Why—Stretches spine and promotes flexibility. A good beginning for backward rolls.

How—Place your baby on her back. Holding her legs, one in each hand, roll her legs back over her head, but do not force her feet all the way to the floor. Your baby's flexibility will improve gradually so that in time her feet will touch the floor. Repeat, trying to maintain eye contact.

9. TUG OF WAR

Why—Strengthens the arms, chest, and hand grip.

How—Place your baby on her back. You may use any of the following pieces of equipment for this exercise: a rattle with a handle, the leg or arm of a soft doll, a ribbon or rope tied in a circle, or a dowel. Encourage your baby to get a good grip on the object you give her. As she holds it, her arms will be flexed near her chest. First pull the object up so your child's arms are extended. Then let your child gently pull her arms back to the near-chest position. As you pull the object up you will meet with resistance, and your baby will love it.

10. ROLLING OVER

Why—Good overall exercise. Preparation for turning over.

How—Place your child flat on his back. Face your baby and with your hand stretch his right arm out on the floor above his head. Hold his left leg with your right hand. Roll him over toward his right side until he is on his tummy. Then put his right arm next to his chest, causing his shoulders to protrude out and up a little. Roll him over toward his left side until he is on his back. Repeat, working opposite sides.

11. LEGS UP

Why—Strengthens stomach, legs, chest, and back.

How—Place your baby on his tummy. Place your hands under his thighs and gently lift his legs off the floor several inches. Your baby may tip forward onto his nose. Don't worry. Soon he will learn to turn his head to the side. As your child gets used to the exercise, slightly increase the height to which you raise his legs.

12. LEG KICKS

Why—Workout for the legs and lower back.

How—Place your baby on her stomach. Hold her legs and raise one as you lower the other, alternating in a gentle rhythm. Before you begin, place a toy in front of your child to give her something to watch and to encourage reaching.

13. BACK STRETCH

Why—Workout for upper back, chest, and shoulders.

How—Place your baby on her stomach with her arms on the floor above her head. Face your baby and grasp her wrists. Lift her upper torso, then lower it to the floor. Keep the hips on the floor. Maintain eye contact and give lots of positive praise. Repeat several times. Now go behind your baby and hold her legs down gently. Watch her try to lift her upper body. Work up to several repetitions.

14. WHEELBARROW

Why—Strengthens arms and back and chest and stomach muscles.

How—Place your baby on his tummy with his hands flat on the floor underneath his shoulders. Place one of your hands under his chest and the other under his tummy. Lift his hips and chest off the floor so his weight rests on his hands and arms. Hold this position for the count of two and then lower him to the floor. Repeat, increasing the amount of time spent in the lifted position.

15. CATERPILLAR

Why—Workout for arms and legs. Prepares the child for crawling.

How—Place your baby on his tummy. Tuck his feet up close to his body. Hold your hand against the soles of his feet. He will move by straightening his legs. Work up to several repetitions.

16. TUMMY TIGHTENER

Why—Strengthens the abdominal muscles and lower back muscles.

How—Place your child flat on her back. Using your finger, make several straight lines on your baby's bare tummy around the navel. With each stroke of your finger the baby's abdominal muscles will contract. Repeat, using a slow rhythm and letting the baby react to each stroke.

17. SIT-UPS TO STAND-UPS

Why—Strengthens the stomach and legs and helps baby find her balance. Aids in preparing the child for sitting and standing.

How—Place your baby on her back. Place her fingers around your thumbs or around a dowel and cover her fingers with your hands. Place her feet against your leg or knee to give her a place to push. Slowly pull the baby to a sitting position. (If she is unable to support her head, help her by holding both her hands in one of yours and supporting her neck and head with the other hand.) After she reaches a sitting position, slowly pull her to a standing position. From standing, lower her back to a sitting position and then back to a lying position. Work up to several repetitions.

18. THE SWING

Why—Workout for the upper body and arms. Helps improve the hand grip. Your baby will love this one, but go slowly at first.

How—Place your baby's hands around a broomstick, dowel, or your fingers. (Eventually try all three.) Place your hands over his to prevent him from letting go. Slowly lift him off the floor a little, letting him hang a few seconds. Then gently begin to swing him back and forth. Return him to the floor and shake his arms a little to release tension and relax the muscles. If your child is unable to hold his own head up, use one of your hands over both of your child's hands and place your other hand behind his neck to support his neck muscles. At first have your baby's face toward yours for added security, but later try this exercise with his face away from yours.

19. FLYING HIGH

Why—Workout for the back and neck muscles.

How—Lie down on your back with your knees bent and your lower legs up off the floor. Place your baby face down on your raised shins, holding his hands out to the sides. Slowly lift your legs so the baby is raised up higher. Hold the position a few seconds, and then lower your legs so your baby is lowered. Repeat this up and down movement, working up to several times.

20. ROW-A-BOAT

Why—Helps exercise the back, leg, and stomach muscles.

How—Place your baby on the floor on her back. Sit facing her so your spread legs meet. Place your legs gently over your baby's outstretched legs. If your baby can support her head, hold her hands. If she cannot support her head, hold your hands around her head and shoulders. Gently pull her to a sitting position and then lower her back to the floor. Try rocking to each side. The following song, which your child will love, will help you to maintain a rhythm:

Row, row, row your boat,
Gently down the stream.
Merrily, merrily, merrily, merrily,
Life is but a dream!

21. IRONING BOARD PLAY

Why—Helps in movement and balance.

How—Get out the ironing board and blow off the dust. Position the narrow end of the board securely on a chair seat. Place the other end on the floor. Now try to slide your baby down the board in a number of positions: head first, feet first, on her tummy, on her back, sitting up. Then try the Caterpillar exercise described earlier, helping your baby push her way up the slide.

22. FOOT FLEX

Why—Stretches heel tendons, makes instep flexible, and strengthens arch.

How—Place your baby on his back. Hold his ankle in one of your hands and with your other thumb, push the ball of his foot upward to full stretch. Then, still holding the ankle, press down on the top of his foot to point his toes. Repeat with the baby's other foot.

CHAPTER TWELVE

Trends in Fathering

Traditionally, our society has had a rather narrow perception of the father's role in the family. His responsibility to his children was viewed as primarily procreative and economic. Today, however, the paternal role has evolved to include such qualities as tenderness, warmth, and compassion. In many respects, the evolution of this role involves changes so fundamental that it is not enough merely to switch genders in describing parenting roles. That is, what fathers do now and will do in the future cannot be seen simply as a takeover of the duties formerly carried out by mothers. It is not enough to say that the "new father" is simply a reincarnation of the historical father, with certain "motherly" duties added.

Today's father is redefining himself and is emerging as a strong, caring, competent partner in the business of the human family. In the process, he is discovering that he can receive emotional satisfaction, psychological gratification, and genuine pleasure from his expanded role. He is learning that not only do his children and his partner benefit from his involvement, but that he, too, feels fulfilled.

This chapter will consider the implications of this emerging paternal role by exploring some recent trends in fathering.

HOSPITAL PRACTICES

Hospitals have begun to acknowledge the important position of the father, with recent obstetrical alternatives representing a growing recognition that childbirth involves the whole family. This recognition, coupled with the movement to view birth as a normal, healthy occurrence, has resulted in something called family-centered care. Most aspects of family-centered care provide for the father's involvement.

In the last twenty-five years an increasing number of hospitals have opened their labor and delivery room doors to prepared fathers. As fathers' involvement has expanded, we have witnessed the introduction of a wide range of alternatives to traditional obstetrical procedures. For example, some hospitals now allow the father to be present in the delivery room for non-emergency cesarean births. In the case of normal vaginal deliveries, some couples now choose to use methods suggested by Dr. Leboyer, a French obstetrician who argues for gentle births. One of Leboyer's methods calls for the father to bathe the baby in warm water just minutes after its birth. He also suggests that the father offer the newborn a gentle body massage as the baby lies on the mother's abdomen.

Alternative settings for childbirth have also been made available. Home births offer the ultimate in family involvement, requiring the father's active participation in a setting where he is comfortable. Hospitals are responding to the trend toward home births by offering more homelike settings within the hospital (birthing rooms) or in an adjoining building (maternity centers). In these comfortable settings the couple may progress through labor with little obstetrical intervention. Because the woman is not confined to a delivery table, the father may be closer to her and to the birth. In some centers the father is invited to cut the umbilical cord, and it is the father who hands the newborn to the mother.

Another innovation in family-centered hospital care involves removing the father from "visitor" status and making him welcome for most of the day. Some hospitals allow the father to stay with mother and baby around the clock if facilities are available. Other hospitals now arrange for the new parents to have a candlelit champagne and steak dinner following the birth. In some hospitals fathers can continue to eat meals with their partners during the hospital stay, either by making arrangements with the dietary department or by bringing meals from home.

Rooming-in has also become fairly common. With this hospital policy, a mother may have her newborn in the room with her around the clock, or for any part of the day and night. Thus the visiting father has unlimited access to his new child. Furthermore, he can become involved in caring for the newborn, as nurses offer instruction in baby care. Where rooming-in is not available or is not chosen, fathers may be welcomed into the well-baby nursery where they can pick up their child and bring him to the mother's room. In intensive care nurseries, there may be a twenty-four hour accessibility policy so that fathers can watch, photograph, or help care for their premature infant or their newborn who requires close medical observation.

The concept of family orientation is common to all the new obstetrical alternatives. If men were not requesting such changes and options, if they were not taking advantage of these alternatives, and if new fathers were not reporting pleasure and satisfaction with their increasing involvement, it is likely that we would not be seeing the remarkable changes in hospital policy that have taken place.

FATHERS RECOGNIZE THEIR ABILITY TO NURTURE

In the past, most parenting activities were assigned according to sexual stereotypes. Thus, it was understood that mother would feed, bathe, and comfort the child; father would support, protect, and discipline the child. We now have come to understand that the ability to nurture a child is not sex-linked. Rather, it is a trait that is linked to our being human. Your interest in caring for and responding to your child is related to the fact that you are a human parent. There have always been some fathers who understood this principle and behaved accordingly. Other men, however, either did not recognize their nurturing tendencies or repressed them because this was encouraged by the society in which they lived.

Fortunately, society has begun to accept the nurturing image of the father. In many circles it is no longer unusual for a man to feed, burp, diaper, or bathe a baby. Often it is the father who is able to soothe a fussy baby or rock the over-tired toddler to sleep. These men express irritation or impatience with the caricature of the bumbling, awkward father who must be rescued from his own child by the all-knowing, capable female. As a matter of fact, the notions that fathers are uninterested in newborn infants, or are less competent than mothers to care for them, have been shown to be completely false.[86] When given the opportunity to care for newborns, fathers are as capable as mothers and demonstrate the same nurturing abilities and tendencies. One new father reported,

> *I had heard that babies were really a drag—really boring—until they were about six months old. I'm living with my two-month-old daughter and I've found her amazing and entertaining from the beginning. It's incredible how responsive she is. What were those other fathers doing for the first six months that they missed it all?*

It seems that as men recognize and accept this nurturing role, they become more involved in fathering. They also feel more competent and more comfortable. A father of three young children told us,

> *It's always been important to me to be good at what I do. Well, now being a father is one of the things I do. . . and I'm good at it. Pajamas aren't always snapped on right, but I know which books are the favorites and which kid likes which yogurt. And I'm the one who always has had the best luck getting Michael to sleep. I seem to have developed a superior rocking*

> *technique. I find it satisfying that my wife, and even my friends, view me as competent in dealing with my children.*

Our society has responded to this evolution of the paternal role, and today a father's ability to care for his child is admired as a manly activity.

SOCIAL, ECONOMIC, AND LEGAL ASPECTS

At all levels of society, fathering is emerging as an important and definable part of the care and sustenance of a family. In recognition of this, high schools are offering "parenting" classes for male and female teen-agers who frequently have little chance to be part of a newborn's life. In these classes teen-agers discuss the realities of marriage and family, as well as the responsibilities involved in having children. Some high school programs include a "practicum" in which teen-agers of both sexes help in a day-care center and learn what child care really entails.

Prenuptial discussions, whether organized formally by religious institutions or organized informally among couples, are including exploration of what the husbands' and wives' lives will be like if they have children. Support groups are springing up around the country to aid fathers in defining their roles and expanding their participation. Local YMCAs, community associations, colleges, adult education programs, and "parenting" groups are offering courses for fathers only and for couples. Child-rearing books have made great strides in including fathers throughout the texts and in pictures.

Economic conditions and the women's movement have also had a tremendous impact on fathering. Women who had full-time jobs prior to pregnancy often resume their jobs shortly after giving birth. Their reasons may be financial, psychological, or related to the demands of a developing career. This tendency places a natural pressure upon concerned fathers to share the parenting responsibilities and become more active in child care so that the child can receive the attention he or she needs and deserves. In some families that opt for full-time parenting, couples decide that the mother (who may be earning more than the father) will return to work, and the father will care for the children.

Current legal activity reflects this growing concern for active fathering. In divorce cases, courts no longer automatically award child custody to mothers. Rather, they seek to give custody to the best parent for the child. Similarly, child support may not always fall to the male if, in fact, the woman is the breadwinner. Adoption agencies now recognize that the single father can be an appropriate adopting parent. In addition, single men are being given the opportunity to be foster parents.

BALANCING WORK AND FAMILY LIFE

Fathers are growing dissatisfied with being regarded solely as the family breadwinners. For a growing number of men, such a role is far too confining. They choose instead to be included in the family in a significant manner. They wish to know their own children firsthand. These men realize the financial benefits available to those who devote themselves to "climbing the ladder of success," but many are beginning to question the hidden costs of such "success." They are insisting that finding success in their personal lives also matters—to themselves, to their families, and to society. As one father remarked, "It's unfortunate and unfair that generally a man's success is measured in terms of the money he makes."

It's clear that some men recognize other measures of achievement. A father of two preschoolers told us:

> *For the most part, I work a forty-hour week. Rarely do I go into the office on a Saturday. I purposely try to limit my hours. When I do have to work longer hours or travel, my children really miss me. I'm glad they don't take my absence in stride. I'm glad it disrupts them. It tells me they need me, they like to have me around, they count on being with me for part of each day. Of course, the other side of that coin is the fact that I need them and I miss them, too, when my schedule interferes with our usual routines.*

As the definitions of masculinity and feminity have broadened, there has been increased social acceptability of vocational changes. More and more men are taking paternity leave in order to be with their partners during childbirth and in the days or weeks following. Where paternity leave is not yet available, men have taken annual leave or have saved their vacation days for this purpose. Some men are seeking out more flexible jobs or are arranging their hours so that they can play a larger role in parenting. Often, both mother and father work part-time, sharing financial responsibility and parenting activities.

Even those fathers who remain in traditional work situations are making efforts to be available to their families. One young father made the following observation:

> *It's not just work that can keep a man from his family. I know some men who are jogging, golfing, fishing, or*

hunting when they're not working. I am envious of the time they have for their personal recreation, but I'm not envious of the relationships they have with their wives or their children. I guess you just have to make some choices.

There are growing numbers of men who arrange to take time off for a child's doctor appointment, for parent-teacher conferences, or to accompany their child's class on a field-trip. In addition, these men find it important to give their children a sense of what daddy does outside the home and therefore will bring a son or daughter to their place of work on occasion. Such men are requesting, sometimes demanding, and often receiving more on-the-job flexibility and understanding in order to balance the complicated demands of employment and fathering.

Today a man may not be able—nor may he wish—to abandon his role of parent when he goes to work each day. Many fathers reject employment situations that require a negation of parenthood. Indeed, it seems that the vitality of the modern family depends upon this commitment.

THE BENEFITS OF ACTIVE FATHERING

The trends in parenting today seem to center around the establishment of flexibility and balance in family roles. Active fathering has been hailed by both ends of the political/cultural spectrum. For the more liberated, father involvement means recognition of the needs and talents of both parents, resulting in shared responsibility and shared pleasures in the job of raising a family. For the more conservative, active fathering is hailed as the rebirth and reaffirmation of the family unit, an institution whose future had seemed uncertain. Fathering probably would not be evolving in such a manner were it not fundamentally enjoyable and rewarding for those men who are willing to grow in this role. The experience expands, intensifies, and enriches the father's relationships with his partner and his children.

The father who shares pregnancy and childbirth with his partner has already begun to deepen his involvement with her. If he then proceeds to share in the care and nurturing of their child, he finds himself participating in a real partnership, one that solidifies his relationship with her and with his child. His support may be the major factor in the woman's successful breastfeeding; his participation in the family is likely to reduce those feelings of postpartum alienation many men and women report; his willingness to communicate with his partner about their new situation may ease the adjustment period for both adults. Men and women are now understanding these subtleties and are discovering the value of their shared involvement.

Beyond the deepening relationship with his partner, active fathering involves the man in a brand new relationship—the one with his child. Men are choosing to make this father-child bond deep, meaningful, and central in their lives. They are coming to know their children intimately and, as a result, are sought out by their sons and daughters. These fathers are important in the family, openly loved and needed. Such men take genuine pride in their children's development, for they have had a significant impact upon it.

The father gets to know himself better through his interactions with his child. Many men are realizing they can experience an important developmental step in their own lives by becoming fathers. In taking care of his children and experiencing and sharing their physical and intellectual development, a father grows and develops new ways of viewing the world, ordering priorities, and establishing values. Through active fathering, a man may rediscover interests and pleasures he enjoyed as a child. He may begin to feel that he has a compelling reason for living a healthy, well-balanced life. He may adopt a less stressful lifestyle.

Active parenting needs to be an ongoing commitment, a daily habit practiced for the betterment of one's self and one's family. Once you have become a new father, you will be able to discover for yourself the special joys and frustrations that come with rearing a child. You can make your life as a father rich and rewarding for yourself. Although many aspects of good fathering will come naturally to you, much can be gained from reading and listening. Become informed and remain flexible. If you share with your partner the care and nurturing of your children, you will be enriching and enhancing the life experiences of every member of your family.

APPENDIX I

*Hospital Policies Concerning the Participation of Fathers in Labor and Birth**

If you and your partner are planning a hospital birth and you wish to participate, don't wait until the last minute to find out how your hospital and your physician or midwife stand on the issue. If you discover that the policies are not suited to your needs you will want to take some action, and the sooner the better. If you fail to investigate ahead of time, you may find yourself excluded at the labor room door. Forget the scenario that has you chaining yourself to your partner's bedpost. This is not the best solution; even if the police are not called to issue you a citation for trespassing, you will almost certainly upset the medical staff, yourself, and your partner.

*Authors assisted by John Grad.

In short, couples who do not check out hospital policy in advance risk disappointment and last-minute difficulties.

WHO SETS THE POLICY?

Policies concerning the participation of fathers in labor and birth vary from hospital to hospital. They are developed and changed largely by the obstetricians who comprise the obstetrics staff. This is a logical arrangement since these are the people most familiar with the issues related to childbirth. Generally, staff members from other sections in the hospital will not particularly care what the obstetrics staff members want to do, so long as their decisions are responsible and do not impinge on the workings of the rest of the hospital.

A hospital's policies regarding childbirth may address such issues as whether the hospital allows fathers in the labor and/or delivery rooms, whether a childbirth education course is a prerequisite for a partner's participation, whether fathers may be present for cesarean deliveries, how much access the father (and mother) can have to the baby, and so on.

As long as the proposals proffered by the members of the obstetrics staff exclude radical or controversial components, they are likely to be approved up the bureaucratic line until they become the stated position of the hospital. The larger the hospital, the more complex its bureaucracy tends to be. In a hospital with hundreds of doctors there is an inherent need for some chaos-reducing structure. In a hospital with a very small number of doctors, the hierarchy may not be overly formal.

After policies are formulated by the obstetrics section, they are presented to the executive committee responsible for medical decisions. This committee is composed principally of

YOU AND THE HOSPITAL BUREAUCRACY

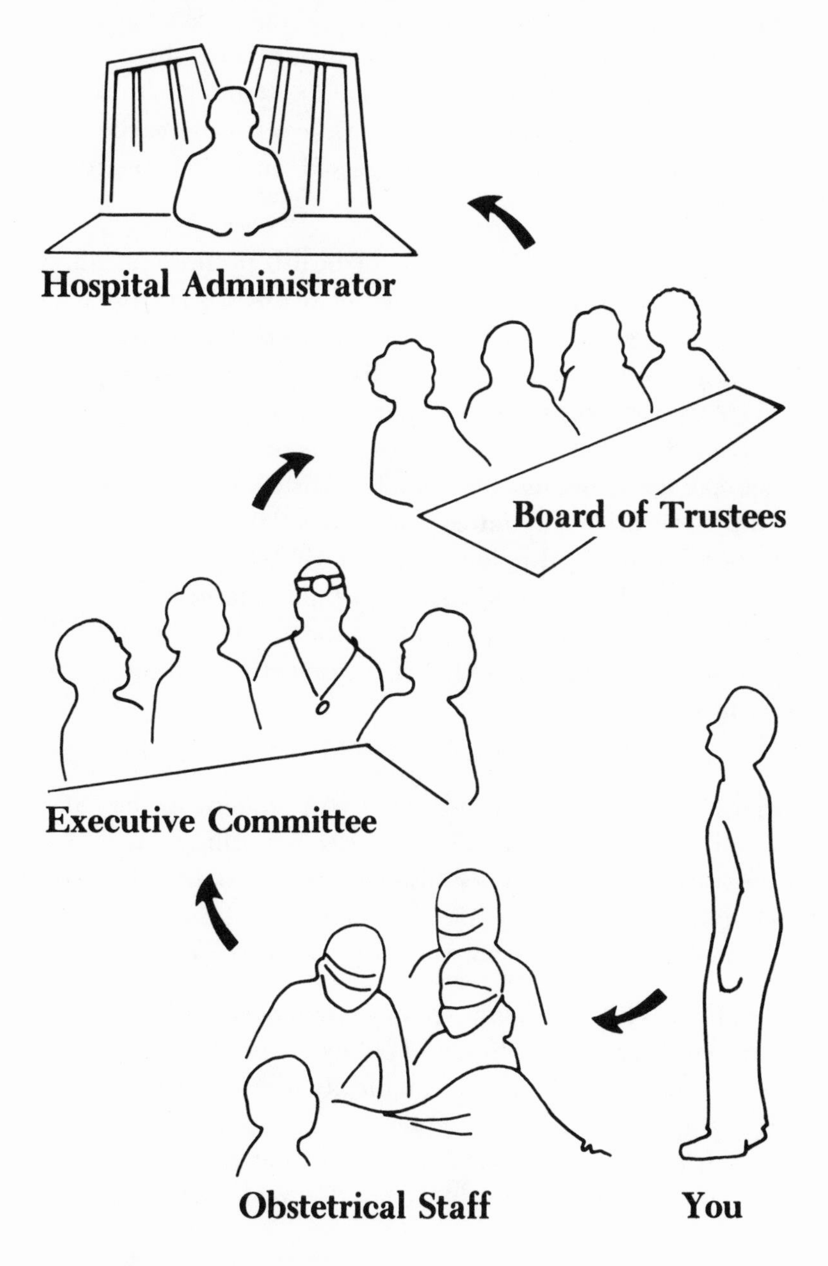

Drawings by Nancy Goer

staff doctors who represent the departments or sections of the hospital. The executive committee recommends what types of services should be offered, what departments should exist in the hospital, and so on. The executive committee's official recommendations usually reflect the consensus reached by the obstetrics section and are passed on to the board of trustees.[87]

The board usually consists of health professionals and lay persons. Officially, the board of trustees is entrusted to make the overall decisions on how the hospital should be run, financed, administered, and the like. It is akin to a corporation's board of directors. The board sets general policy guidelines within which administrators and hospital personnel operate. However, the board of trustees will usually rely on the executive committee's recommendations with respect to hospital medical policy, particularly when the board includes lay persons or when the hospital is large. Generally, the board will focus on overall financial decisions and will rely on its professionals—that is, the executive committee—to set medical policy.

Hospital administrators (who may or may not be physicians) are similar to presidents of corporations in that they usually take their broad directives regarding day-to-day supervision of hospital operations from the board of trustees. Hospital administrators do not make policy, but rather implement the policy set for them by their boards of trustees.

How rigid any hospital policy is and how closely hospital staff members adhere to stated policy are often related to the size of the hospital and the complexity of its bureaucracy. It is not uncommon, for example, that a hospital with a small obstetrics staff will take the position that fathers can participate in childbirth to the extent desired by the individual doctors. That sort of "policy" acknowledges in an informal way what is ultimately true even in larger hospitals: that it is important to accommodate the wishes of the individual practitioner and the parents.

FOUR CONSIDERATIONS

Given the fact that hospital policy, however rigid, generally originates from the obstetrics staff members themselves, it is important to understand the factors considered by these physicians. Usually their thinking will be influenced by four broad types of considerations: the state of the art, consumer demand, economics, and fear of malpractice suits. In some of these areas the consumer can have substantial input.

The State of the Art

The way in which obstetrics is practiced reflects "the state of the art." It goes without saying that physicians vary individually and regionally and display differing degrees of sophistication. For example, physicians in large urban hospitals might use fetal monitors routinely, but monitors would be rare in settings where expensive technology cannot be supported financially and has not been called for by demand.

Thus, the state of the art will influence the sensitivity of doctors to the role that partners play in labor and birth. Some obstetrical practices have less than modern views on this issue. Historically, physicians objected to the father's participation, citing increased risk of infection, concern that the father would interfere in the physician's activities, and concern over the father's alleged inability to cope with certain aspects of medical procedures. Physicians who express concern over these issues may be quite sincere. They probably have not had the positive experience necessary to allay their fears. Typically, traditional attitudes change as doctors become more informed—through formal programs in continuing education, exposure to the practices of younger colleagues familiar with the latest trends, relaxation of their own restrictions, and so on.

Consumer Demand

A doctor, like any other provider of services, cannot exist in a vacuum. The articulated needs of patients will have some impact on what a doctor does. When a doctor's patients are not demanding father participation, the doctor who has never experienced such participation might ignore the whole question. The doctor who has a large clientele who demand father participation will be most apt to respond and take positive action. Younger physicians whose residencies were in hospitals that encouraged father participation, like other physicians who have had experience with it, understand how such participation can aid labor and delivery. These doctors may not need a push from consumers to permit, or even encourage, participation.

Consumer demand has had a significant impact on the acceptance of father participation. Consumer attention has recently shifted toward changing other birth policies. In years to come, we are likely to see wider acceptance of the birthing room, participation of other family members (siblings, grandparents), and more participation of fathers in cesarean deliveries.

Economics

Closely related to consumer demand is the economic factor. Physicians who ignore a steady demand for father participation will quickly find their obstetrical practices dwindling as their clientele shift to more receptive obstetricians or midwives. Humanitarian motivations aside, doctors do practice medicine to make a living. Like any other providers of services, physicians need their clientele and will adapt in order to avoid economic loss.

Fear of Malpractice Suits

Until recently, malpractice suits were not a constant threat to the average doctor. But with increased legal activity and increased consumer sophistication (including the revised view of doctors as providers of services instead of sanctified unapproachables), the threat of a malpractice suit has grown from a minimal nuisance to a very real possibility for any physician.

The great proclivity to sue doctors for mistakes has led to the increased practice of what is called defensive medicine. Defensive medicine does have real benefits: greater scrutiny of medical problems, better recordkeeping, and better medical care as the physicians become directly and publicly accountable for what they do. However, defensive medicine also makes doctors hypersensitive to potential dangers that could lead to some sort of malpractice liability. Some physicians resent having nonprofessional persons looking over their shoulders to observe what they are doing. Some physicians fear that they will be held responsible for any inadvertent harm that may come to the father or to the mother. A whole host of "problems" centers around the presence of the partner in the labor and delivery rooms. The physician's fears tend to suppress innovation and experimentation.

On the other hand, many physicians have realized correctly that the best way to avoid a malpractice case (aside from practicing good medicine) is to have the confidence, trust, and friendship of the patient. These physicians realize that encouraging family participation in labor and delivery has the effect of bringing patients closer to the doctor, and this closeness usually acts to discourage the bitterness that can arise following a problem. One study has shown that in over 45,000 births in which fathers participated, no malpractice suits were brought.[88]

One of the common issues seen in malpractice litigation is the issue of "informed consent." Many doctors have been sued by patients who claimed they suffered injuries that the physician knew to be possible or predictable consequences of a medical procedure, but about which they were given no advance warning. The patients claim that, had they known about the possible hazards, they never would have consented to the procedure. Thus, these patients seek to hold the doctor responsible. The answer to the "informed consent problem" is full clarification of the specific dangers that may arise from a medical procedure. A person about to undergo a procedure officially acknowledges "informed consent" by signing a written consent form. The form may not actually list all the dangers, but it does certify that the potential consequences of a particular procedure have been explained fully.

The same considerations apply to the partner's presence in the labor and delivery rooms. In some hospitals the woman and the man are each asked to sign a written consent form that states that they enter the labor and delivery suite with knowledge of both the complications that might arise and the conditions under which the father would be asked to leave. They also agree to allow particular emergency procedures to be done if necessary, with eviction of the father upon request of the physician. The consent form offers legal protection for the physician and hospital and also serves the useful purpose of ensuring that the couple has received full explanations of the procedures and their possible consequences. Before you sign such a form, make sure you understand what you are signing and that you have been given the explanations specified.

WHAT ARE YOUR LEGAL RIGHTS?

The basic legal rights of fathers, with respect to being in the labor and delivery suite, vary from state to state. Several states have passed specific legislation meant to guarantee the right of fathers to be present. Check with your lawyer or an appropriate childbirth organization in your state to get the latest information. In 1974 an effort was begun to pass such legislation on the federal level, but the legislation died in committee.

There are some jurisdictions in which fathers have an absolute statutory right to be in the labor and delivery suite but might find that for some reason the hospital is not complying with the law. In other instances, there is no law on the subject and the hospital refuses to allow father participation. If you face either of these conflicts, your only recourse is a judicial ruling. When a hospital violates a specific state law providing for father participation, it is generally easy to resolve the matter in court. But where there is no legislation on the subject, as is the case in most states, a lawsuit is more difficult.

Whenever a question is presented to a judge, the two opposing parties must cite some sort of authority, some precedent, to support their positions. In the past, for lack of controversy, the issue of father participation was rarely litigated. Thus there is little support for the father in the "common law" (the body of legal precedent which over the years has defined the relationships of most persons in society). In fact, in the few cases that have reached the courts in recent years, the common law generally sides with the hospital because it views hospitals as corporations whose boards of trustees have the right to dictate policy. Any person who wishes to use the services of a hospital must abide by its rules and regulations or otherwise find another hospital.

Some couples have tried to challenge this notion on the basis of the constitutional "right to privacy." This concept holds that there are certain areas of private personal conduct—the right to use birth control devices, the right to have abortions, and so on—in which the government (and this includes the public and publicly-supported hospital) has no business. Seizing on this theory, several couples trained in prepared childbirth brought suit against a hospital in Indiana, challenging that the hospital's refusal to admit fathers to the delivery room was a violation of their right to privacy.[89] Unfortunately, these couples lost. The judicial opinion, written by now-Supreme Court Justice John Paul Stevens, held that the right to privacy did not extend to protect those couples involved. In this case, the court was unwilling to substitute its judgment for the professional medical judgment of the defendant hospital. When the presence of fathers in the labor and delivery rooms gains wider medical endorsement as being in the best interest of all parties, the judiciary's hands-off attitude might indeed change so that a case of this type may be won.

The same general principle applies in the issue of father participation in cesarean deliveries. A growing number of hospitals now allow fathers to be present for a cesarean birth, but in every case it represents a voluntary policy decision on the part of the hospital and the obstetrician. No case law or legislation supports the expectant parents on this point. Given the general negative reaction of judges to the "easier" question of whether to allow a father to participate in a vaginal birth, it seems highly unlikely that a judge would overrule established hospital policy on cesarean deliveries in favor of the parents. Again, wider medical endorsement and consumer demand offer the best hope for favorable change.

It may be that where judicial rulings against father participation are in force, specific legislation, enacted as a result of the lobbying efforts of a concerned public, will reverse such policies. You may be one of the lobbyists. Remember, hospitals face the economic necessity of filling beds. These days the declining birth rate means that obstetrical wards often have many empty beds. You, as a prepared parent and consumer, may have more power than you realize to bring about change in your local hospitals.

APPENDIX II

Organizations Interested in Childbirth

Alliance for Perinatal Research and Services (APRS)
321 South Pitt Street
Alexandria, Virginia 22314

American Academy of Husband Coached Childbirth
P.O. Box 5224
Sherman Oaks, California 91413

American Academy of Pediatrics
P.O. Box 1034
Evanston, Illinois 60204

American College of Home Obstetrics (ACHO)
Suite 600, 664 North Michigan Avenue
Chicago, Illinois 60611

American College of Nurse Midwives (ACNM)
1012 Fourteenth Street, N.W.
Washington, D.C. 20005

American College of Obstetricians and Gynecologists
1 East Wacker Drive
Chicago, Illinois 60601

American Foundation for Maternal and Child Health, Inc.
30 Beekman Place
New York, New York 10022

American Society for Psychoprophylaxis in Obstetrics (ASPO)
1411 K Street, N.W.
Washington, D.C. 20005

Association for Childbirth at Home, International
16705 Monte Cristo
Cerritos, California 90701

Bananas
6501 Telegraph Avenue
Oakland, California 94609

Caesarean/Support, Education and Concern (C/SEC)
15 Maynard Road
Dedham, Massachusetts 02026

Center for Family Growth
555 Highland Avenue
Cotati, California 94928

Center for Research on Birth and Human Development
Room 105, 2340 Ward Street
Berkeley, California 94705

Childbirth Without Pain Education Association (CWPEA)
20134 Snowden
Detroit, Michigan 48235

Child Study Association of America
9 East 89th Street
New York, New York 10028

Coping with the Overall Pregnancy-Parenting
Experience (COPE)
37 Clarendon Street
Boston, Massachusetts 02116

Home Oriented Maternity Experience (HOME)
511 New York Avenue
Takoma Park, Washington, D.C. 20012

International Childbirth Education Association (ICEA)
P.O. Box 20048
Minneapolis, Minnesota 55420

International Childbirth Education Association (ICEA)
Bookcenter
P.O. Box 20048
Minneapolis, Minnesota 55420

La Leche League International
9616 Minneapolis Avenue
Franklin Park, Illinois 60131

Maternity Center Association
48 East 92nd Street
New York, New York 10028

National Association of Parents and Professionals for Safe Alternatives in Childbirth (NAPSAC)
P.O. Box 267
Marble Hill, Missouri 63764

National Foundation/March of Dimes
P.O. Box 2000
White Plains, New York 10602

National Midwives Association
P.O. Box 163
Princeton, New Jersey

National Self-Help Clearing House
Graduate School and University Center/CUNY
Room 1227, 33 West 42nd Street
New York, New York 10036

Parents Without Partners, Inc.
80 Fifth Street
New York, New York 10011

Planned Parenthood Federation of America
515 Madison Avenue
New York, New York 10022

Society for the Protection of the Unborn Through
Nutrition (SPUN)
Suite 603, 17 North Wabash Street
Chicago, Illinois 60602

Notes

1. T.B. Brazelton, "Effect of Maternal Expectations on Early Infant Behavior," *Early Child Development Care* 2 (1973): 259–73.
2. Suzanne Arms, *Immaculate Deception* (Toronto: Bantam Books, 1979), pp. 10–27.
3. Janet Joseph Lieberman, "Childbirth Practices: From Darkness into Light," *Journal of Obstetric, Gynecologic and Neonatal Nursing* (May/June 1976): 41–45. See also Suzanne Arms, *Immaculate Deception*, pp. 10–27.
4. Arms, *Immaculate Deception*, pp. 10–27.

5. U.S. Department of Health, Education and Welfare, National Center for Health Statistics 27, no. 12 (March 1979).
6. Michael Newton, "Effect of Modern Obstetric Care on the Family," in *The Family—Can It Be Saved?*, eds. Victor C. Vaughn and T. Berry Brazelton (Chicago: Year Book Medical Publishers, Inc., 1976), p. 89.
7. U.S. Department of Health, Education and Welfare, National Center for Health Statistics 27, no. 12 (March 1979).
8. Ibid.
9. Ibid.
10. Peter Mayle, *How to be a Pregnant Father* (Secaucus, New Jersey: Lyle Stuart, Inc., 1977).
11. Elisabeth Bing and Libby Colman, *Making Love During Pregnancy* (New York: Bantam Books, Inc., 1977).
12. T. Berry Brazelton, *Infants and Mothers* (New York: Dell Publishing Company, Inc., 1969), pp. 48-62.
13. Bing, *Making Love*, p. 124.
14. Clellan S. Ford, "A Comparative Study of Human Reproduction," *Yale University Publications in Anthropology*, no. 4 (New Haven: Human Relations Area Files Press, 1964).
15. Ibid.
16. Lieberman, "Childbirth Practices: From Darkness Into Light," 41–45.
17. Richard W. and Dorothy C. Wertz, *Lying-In, A History of Childbirth in America* (New York: The Free Press, 1977), p. 81.

18. Marie S. Brown, "A Cross Cultural Look at Pregnancy, Labor and Delivery," *Journal of Obstetric, Gynecologic and Neonatal Nursing* 5 (1976): 35–38.

19. Wertz and Wertz, *Lying-In*, p. 73.

20. Ibid, p. 81.

21. Elisabeth D. Bing, "Lamaze Childbirth Among the Amish People," *Birth and the Family Journal* 2, no. 2 (1975): 40.

22. Margaret Mead, "Pregnancy, Birth and the Newborn Baby," in *Boston Children's Hospital Medical Center* (New York: Delacorte Press, 1972).

23. Valmai H. Elkins, *The Rights of the Pregnant Parent* (Ottawa: Waxwing Productions, 1976).

24. Leota K. McNall, "Concerns of Expectant Fathers," in *Current Practice in Obstetrics and Gynecology*, eds. Leota K. McNall and Janet T. Galeender (St. Louis: The C.V. Mosby Company, 1976), p. 167.

25. Ibid.

26. Marina Warner, *Alone of All Her Sex* (New York: Alfred A. Knopf, 1976), p. 75.

27. Wolfgang Lederer, *The Fear of Women* (New York: Harcourt Brace Jovanovich, Inc., 1968), p. 33.

28. Wertz and Wertz, *Lying-In*, p. 156.

29. McNall, "Concerns of Expectant Fathers," p. 167.

30. Newton, "Effect of Modern Obstetric Care," p. 89.

31. M. Greenberg and N. Morris, "Engrossment: The Newborn's Impact Upon the Father," *American Journal of Orthopsychiatry* 44 (1974): 520–31.

32. J. Lind, personal communication cited in *Maternal Infant Bonding*, Marshall H. Klaus and John H. Kennell (St. Louis: The C.V. Mosby Company, 1976), p. 65.
33. Suzanne Arms, "Birth Hang-Ups," *Harper's Weekly* 65, no. 3156 (1976): 9.
34. Betsy Lozoff, "Care of the Parent and Human Infant in Newborn Societies," unpublished manuscript, Case Western Reserve Medical School, 1980. See also Robert A. Fein, "Men's Entrance to Parenthood," *The Family Coordinator* (1976): 341–348.
35. Elkins, *The Rights of the Pregnant Parent*, p. 139.
36. Grantly Dick-Read, *Childbirth Without Fear* (New York: Harper and Row, Publishers, 1959).
37. Fernand Lamaze, *Painless Childbirth* (London: Burke, 1958).
38. Majorie Karmel, *Thank You, Dr. Lamaze* (New York: Doubleday and Company, Inc., 1959).
39. Elkins, *The Rights of the Pregnant Parent*, pp. 139–40.
40. J. Kelly, "Effect of Fear Upon Uterine Motility," *American Journal of Obstetrics and Gynecology* 83 (1962): pp. 576-81.
41. Aidan Macfarlane, *The Psychology of Childbirth*, The Developing Child Series (Cambridge, Massachusetts: Harvard University Press, 1977), p. 60.
42. Deborah Tanzer, "Natural Childbirth: Pain or Peak Experience," *Psychology Today* (October 1968): 18–21.
43. John B. Franklin, "Institutional Barriers to the Family," in *The Family—Can It Be Saved?*, eds. Victor C. Vaughan and T. Berry Brazelton (Chicago: Year Book Medical Publishers, Inc., 1976), p. 108.

44. Arms, "Birth Hang-Ups," p. 9.

45. Elkins, *The Rights of the Pregnant Parent*, p. 133.

46. K. Standley, "Local-Regional Anesthesia During Childbirth," *Science* 86 (1974): 634–35.

47. Elkins, *The Rights of the Pregnant Parent*, p. 50.

48. H.R. Gordon, "Fetal Bradycardia After Paracervical Block," *New England Journal of Medicine* 279 (1968): 910–14.

49. Elkins, *The Rights of the Pregnant Parent*, p. 56.

50. J. Wapner, "Attitudes, Feelings, and Behaviors of Expectant Fathers Attending Lamaze Classes," *Birth and Family Journal* 3, no. 1 (1976): 13.

51. Greenberg and Morris, "Engrossment: The Newborn's Impact Upon the Father," 520–31.

52. Ibid.

53. Elkins, *The Rights of the Pregnant Parent*, pp. 16–17.

54. Jackie Staigers, personal communication.

55. Frank Pedersen et al. "Obstetrical Procedures and Practices: Behavioral Outcomes." Presented by Martha Zaslow at the Meetings of the Society for Research in Child Development, San Francisco, California, 1979.

56. L. Waletzky, "Husbands' Problems with Breastfeeding," *American Journal of Orthopsychiatry* 49 (1979): 349–52.

57. Ibid.

58. R. Emde, J. Swedberg, and B. Suzuki, "Human Wakefulness and Biological Rhythms after Birth," *Archives of General Psychiatry* 32 (1975): 780–83.

59. C. Goren, M. Sarty, and P.Y.K. Wu, "Visual Following and Pattern Discrimination of Face-like Stimuli by Newborn Infants," *Pediatrics* 56 (1975): 544–49.

60. R. Eisenberg et al., "Auditory Behavior in the Human Neonate: A Preliminary Report," *Journal of Speech and Hearing Research* 7 (1964): 245–69.

61. P. Eimas et al., Work in progress. (Unpublished, Brown University, 1975).

62. W.S. Condon and L.W. Sander, "Neonate Movement Is Synchronized with Adult Speech: Interactional Participation and Language Acquisition," *Science* 183 (1974): 99–101.

63. Marshall H. Klaus and John H. Kennell, *Maternal-Infant Bonding* (St. Louis, Missouri: The C.V. Mosby Company, 1976), p. 73.

64. T. Berry Brazelton, "Behavioral Competence of the Newborn Infant," *Seminars in Perinatology* 3 (1979): 35–44.

65. J.A. Macfarlane, "Olfaction in the Development of Social Preferences in the Human Neonate," in *Parent-Infant Interaction, Ciba Foundation Symposium 33 (new series)* (Amsterdam: Elsevier, Associated Scientific Publishers, 1975), pp. 103–117.

66. Brazelton, "Behavioral Competence of the Newborn Infant," p. 39.

67. Peter H. Wolfe, "Observations on Newborn Infants," *Psychosomatic Medicine* 21 (1959): 110–18.

68. T. Berry Brazelton, *Neonatal Behavioral Assessment Scale*, Clinics in Developmental Medicine No. 50 (Philadelphia: J.B. Lippincott Co., 1973), p. 5.

69. Z.L. Cassel and L.W. Sander, "Neonatal Recognition Processes and Attachment: The Masking Experiment." Paper presented at the Society for Research in Child Development, Denver, 1975.

70. American Academy of Pediatrics, "Breast-feeding," *Pediatrics* 62 (1978): 591–601.

71. Ibid.

72. N. Newton, "Psychologic Differences Between Breast and Bottle Feeding," *American Journal of Clinical Nutrition*, 24 (1971): 994.

73. Betsy Lozoff et al., "The Mother-Newborn Relationship: Limits of Acceptability," *Journal of Pediatrics* 91 (1977): 1–12.

74. Dana Raphael, *The Tender Gift: Breastfeeding* (Englewood Cliffs, N.J.: Prentice-Hall, Inc., 1973).

75. L. Waletzky, "Husbands' Problems with Breastfeeding," pp. 349–52.

76. H. Harlow, "The Nature of Love," *American Psychologist* 10 (1975): 149–53.

77. R. Parke and S. O'Leary, "Father-Mother-Infant Interaction in the Newborn Period: Some Findings, Some Observations and Some Unresolved Issues," In *The Developing Individual in a Changing World, Vol. II*, eds. K. Riegel and J. Meacham (The Hague: Mouton, 1976).

78. A.F. Korner and E.B. Thoman, "Visual Alertness in Neonates as Evoked by Maternal Care," *Journal of Experimental Child Psychology* 10 (1970): 67.

79. Lee Salk and Rita Kramer, *How to Raise a Human Being* (New York: Random House, 1969), p. 65.

80. P. Karlberg, "The Adaptive Changes in the Immediate Postnatal Period with Particular Reference to Respiration," *Journal of Pediatrics* 56 (1960): 585–604.

81. S. Bell and M. Ainsworth, "Infant Crying and Maternal Responsiveness," *Child Development* 43 (1972): 1171–90.

82. Tine Thevenin, *The Family Bed* (Minneapolis: Tine Thevenin, 1976).

83. Brazelton, "Behavioral Competence of the Newborn Infant," p. 42.

84. Margaret Wise Brown, *Goodnight Moon* (New York: Harper & Row, Publishers, 1947).

85. Margaret Wise Brown, *The Runaway Bunny* (New York: Harper & Row, Publishers, 1942).

86. Ross D. Parke, "Family Interaction in the Newborn Period: Some Findings, Some Observations, and Some Unresolved Issues," in *The Developing Individual in a Changing World, Vol. II*, eds. K. Riegel and J. Meacham (The Hague: Mouton, 1976).

87. This governing body may have a different "official name" depending on local custom and law, for example, "board of directors" or "board of visitors." Similarly, the executive committee may be referred to as the "medical staff" or by another term signifying the official body of health professionals who make medical decisions and recommendations for the hospital.

88. Fitzgerald v. Porter Memorial Hospital, 523 F. 2d 716 (7th Cir. 1975).

89. Fitzgerald v. Porter Memorial Hospital.

Glossary

Abruptio placenta—A premature detachment of the placenta from the uterine wall.

Afterbirth—Another term for the placenta and membranes that are delivered after the baby is born.

Afterpains—Pains that occur as the uterus contracts after birth in an effort to retain its original muscle tone. First-time mothers usually do not experience afterpains.

Amniocentesis—A procedure in which some amniotic fluid is withdrawn from the bag of waters by inserting a needle through the abdomen and uterine wall. The test can be used to determine Rh problems, hereditary disorders, and gestational age of the fetus.

Amnion—The innermost layer of two membranes that surround the fetus to form the bag of waters. The outermost layer is called the *chorion.*

Amniotic fluid—The transparent fluid that fills the amniotic sac or bag of waters. It maintains an even temperature for the fetus and allows it to move around easily. The fluid is constantly being replenished, with about 500 to 1000 milliliters of fluid being expelled during delivery.

Amniotic sac—The transparent "bag of waters" that is filled with amniotic fluid. The sac grows as the baby grows.

Amniotomy—Another term for the procedure in which the doctor or midwife artificially breaks the bag of waters with a sterile instrument.

Analgesic—A class of drugs that works to alleviate pain. One common analgesic used in labor is Demerol.

Anesthetic agents—The group of drugs that cause the loss of sensation. They can be either general (producing unconsciousness), regional (numbing a specific set of nerves, as with an epidural), or local (deadening pain in a small, specific area).

Anoxia—A lack of oxygen, sometimes occurring in newborns in distress.

Antenatal—The time before birth.

Antiseptic—A liquid preparation used on the skin to inhibit the growth of bacteria.

APGAR—A score given to a newborn at one minute and again at five minutes after birth to assess the health of the baby. The score is based on five criteria: heartrate, muscle tone, respiratory effort, reflex irritability, and skin color. Ten is the highest possible score.

Bag of waters—A term synonomous with amniotic sac.

Barbiturate—A type of drug sometimes used in very early labor or in false labor to induce drowsiness in the mother and allow her to sleep. Common barbiturates are Nembutal and Seconal. If taken close to delivery, these drugs can have a negative effect on the fetus.

Birth canal—A term synonomous with vagina; the canal through which the baby passes during the pushing stage of labor.

Bloody show (or "*Show*")—A vaginal discharge composed of mucous flecked with blood; can occur at the time the mucous plug is lost and can continue throughout labor.

Bonding—A period of attachment formation between parent and baby that occurs during a sensitive period soon after delivery. It includes the touching, smelling, seeing, and stroking parents go through with their newborn.

Bradycardia—A slow heartbeat (below 120 beats per minute).

Braxton-Hicks contractions—Intermittent and usually painless contractions of the uterus during the mid to late months of pregnancy. These contractions allow the uterus to "warm up" for labor.

Breech—Position of the baby in the uterus when the buttocks or feet are entering the birth canal first at the time of delivery.

Buccal—The oral administration of medication, often Pitocin.

Catheter—A small tube used to collect urine directly from the bladder.

Caudal block—A regional type of anesthesia given in the lower spinal area.

Centimeters—A unit of measure used to describe the progress of the dilating cervix. Dilation is complete at ten centimeters.

Cephalo-pelvic disproportion (CPD)—A phenomenon of labor where the baby's head (cephalo) does not fit through the mother's pelvis (pelvic). This is suspected if the baby's head does not descend properly in the pelvis and can be confirmed by x-ray pelvimetry. It usually means the baby will be delivered by cesarean delivery.

Cervix—The necklike, narrow end of the uterus opening into the vagina. It must be open during labor to allow the baby to pass through to the birth canal.

Cesarean delivery—A type of delivery that occurs through an abdominal incision. There are several reasons why a mother might need a cesarean delivery, including: cephalo-pelvic disproportion (see above), improper position of baby, failure of labor to progress, medical complications, previous cesarean, or fetal distress.

Chorion—The outer of the two membranes composing the amniotic sac.

Colostrum—The yellowish fluid secreted by the breasts in small quantities during pregnancy and for two or three days following delivery. This is "early" milk.

"*Complete*"—A term used by hospital personnel to indicate that the cervix is completely dilated to ten centimeters.

Contraction—A regular tightening and shortening of the uterine muscles during labor causing the effacement and dilation of the cervix and contributing to the downward and outward descent of the baby.

Cord prolapse (also known as *Prolapsed cord*)—A situation in which the umbilical cord slips down into the birth canal before the fetus does. This problem usually necessitates a cesarean delivery.

Crowning—The time when the first part of the baby (usually the crown of the head) is visible at the vaginal opening and no longer slips back out of sight between contractions.

Demerol—The trade name for meperidine, a narcotic analgesic used for pain relief during labor.

Dilatation (also called *Dilation*)—The gradual opening of the cervix, accomplished by uterine contractions, to permit passage of the baby out of the uterus and into the birth canal.

Dystocia—A term referring to a difficult labor.

Eclampsia—An advanced stage of toxemia which may occur late in pregnancy or during labor where the mother's blood pressure rises alarmingly and convulsions may occur.

Edema—A swelling of a part of the body, usually the feet, hands, and face, resulting from fluid retention.

Effacement—A thinning out and drawing up of the cervix to permit full dilation. This usually occurs simultaneously with dilation. It is expressed in terms of a percentage (for example, 90 percent effaced).

Effleurage—A light, fingertip massage of the abdomen that aids relaxation of the abdominal muscles.

Engagement—A term indicating that the presenting part of the baby has secured itself in the pelvic inlet and is in position to pass through the pelvic bones.

Engorgement—An excessive fullness of the breasts due to the initiation of milk production.

Epidural block—A type of regional anesthesia injected into the epidural space in the lower spinal area.

Episiotomy—An incision made into the perineum prior to delivery to prevent lacerations and to facilitate delivery.

Expulsion—The second stage of labor, comprising the actual forcing out of the baby after complete dilatation of the cervix. It is facilitated by the pushing efforts of the mother.

Fetus—A medical term used to denote the baby from the third month of pregnancy to birth.

Fontanelle—The space at the meeting of the skull bones where the "soft spot" of the baby's head can be felt. The space closes after a few months of life and hardens over.

Forceps—The obstetrical instrument occasionally used to aid in delivery.

Fundus—The upper portion of the uterus.

Gravida—A term used to designate the number of times a woman has been pregnant. A first pregnancy is called Gravida I.

Hemorrhage—An excessive amount of bleeding.

Hyaline membrane disease (also known as *RDS* or *Respiratory Distress Syndrome*)—A respiratory disease that affects premature infants.

Hypertension—A term synonymous with high blood pressure.

Hyperventilation—A possible side effect of improper breathing during labor, signaling that breathing is either too fast or too deep. Hyperventilation leads to excessive depletion of carbon dioxide, manifested by dizziness and by tingling in the extremities.

Hypotension—An abnormally low blood pressure.

Hypoxia—A condition in which the infant in utero is not getting enough oxygen. This often leads to fetal distress.

Induction—The artificial initiation of labor. This can be accomplished by rupturing the membranes, by an enema, or by medication known as Pitocin.

In utero—Latin for "in the uterus."

Involution—The return of the reproductive organs to the normal, nonpregnant state.

Labor—The entire process of delivery from the onset of contractions to the expulsion of the baby.

Laceration—A tear in the perineal tissues or muscles.

Lactation—The process of producing and secreting milk.

L&D (Labor and Delivery)—The term used to refer to that portion of the hospitals where babies are born.

Lightening—A shifting of the baby and uterus downward into the pelvis, noticed by a change in the contour of the abdomen.

Lochia—A discharge of blood, mucous, and tissue from the uterus after birth. Changes color from red to brown to pale yellow.

Meconium—The dark green or black substance in the baby's intestines that passes through as bowel movements for the first few days after birth. It is composed of digested amniotic fluid.

Membranes—The membranous sac that contains fetus, placenta, and amniotic fluid; also known as the amniotic sac or "bag of waters."

Molding—The shaping of the fetal head as it adapts itself to the pelvic canal during the second stage of labor.

Multipara—A woman giving birth for the second or subsequent time.

Neonate—A newborn baby.

Occiput—The back of the head.

Os—In obstetrics, a term which refers to the opening of the cervix (i.e., "the cervical os").

Oxytocin—The hormone used to induce uterine contractions, either to stimulate labor or to encourage involution of the uterus following birth.

Paracervical block—A type of regional anesthesia used during the first stage of labor. It is injected into the cervical nerve branch located at the junction of the cervix and vagina.

Perineum—The floor of the pelvis.

Pitocin—The trade name for synthetic oxytocin, sometimes referred to as "Pit."

Placenta—The organ that exchanges oxygen, nutrients, and wastes between mother and fetus. It also screens some unnecessary substances from the fetus and produces hormones to support pregnancy.

Placenta previa—A condition in which the placenta lies over the cervix rather than high up in the uterus. The primary symptom is painless bleeding, which usually develops during the final trimester. Placenta previa is classified as complete, partial, or marginal depending on how much of the cervix is covered. For complete or partial placenta previa, cesarean delivery is usually necessary, but in marginal cases vaginal delivery is sometimes possible.

Posterior presentation—A term used to indicate that the baby is descending through the birth canal in a face up rather than a face down position. It is not serious enough to be considered a complication of labor but may be related to "back labor" in which the discomfort from contractions is felt in the lower back.

Postpartum—Latin for "after birth."

Precipitate labor—A very fast labor and delivery, usually occurring in less than three hours.

Pre-eclampsia—A toxemia of pregnancy that occurs in the third trimester. The main symptoms are hypertension, weight gain, edema, and the presence of protein in the urine. The cause is unknown.

Premature—A category referring to a live infant born at less than thirty-six weeks gestion or weighting under 2500 grams (or five pounds, eight ounces).

Prep—A common term for shaving of the pubic hair. Preps (preparation for delivery) can be complete, half, or mini depending on what the doctor orders.

Presenting part—The part of the baby (usually the head) that is lowest in the pelvis.

Primigravida—A woman pregnant for the first time.

Pudendal block—A regional anesthesia used at the time of delivery to numb the mother's external genitalia.

Puerpium—The period after delivery during which involution of the uterus occurs.

RH Factor—A substance discovered through experimentation with rhesus monkeys. This substance is present in the blood of most people; people who have it are RH+ (positive) and those lacking it are RH− (negative). If the mother is RH− and the father is RH+, a problem can arise because the baby in utero is usually (but not always) RH+. When a positive baby is inside a negative mother, the mother's immune system can make antibodies in her blood that could hurt the baby she is carrying or future babies. Since the sensitization to RH factors occurs most frequently at the time of delivery, an injection of a substance called RHOGAM soon after birth can prevent this process and act to protect future babies. Depending on the time of occurrence, RHOGAM also may have to be given after abortions or miscarriages.

Rooming-in—The practice of having the baby stay in the mother's hospital room for all or most of the day and night, if so desired.

Saddle block—A type of regional anesthesia that numbs those areas of the body that would come in contact with a saddle when riding a horse. It is usually given at the time of delivery in the lower spine.

Sonogram—A picture of the baby made by reflected sound waves through the mother's abdomen. This technique is used to detect the presence of twins, to detect placenta previa, to assess fetal development, or for other diagnostic purposes.

Souffle—A blowing sound heard with a stethoscope held over the pregnant abdomen; it is simultaneous with the woman's pulse and is caused by blood rushing past the maternal side of the placenta.

Station—The position of the presenting part of the fetus in relation to the mother's pelvic bones. Expressed in numbers from "minus four" (still high) to "plus four" (at the vaginal opening). At station zero, the head is engaged.

Striae—The pink or purplish lines on the abdomen or breasts caused by the stretching of the skin during pregnancy. After delivery, striae gradually become white and appear shiny. Also known as "stretch marks."

Symphysis pubis—The joint at the center and front of the pelvis.

Term—The natural duration of pregnancy, 280 days.

Toxemia—An abnormal bodily reaction to pregnancy characterized by edema, hypertension, and protein in the urine, and occurring after the twentieth week of pregnancy; often referred to as pre-eclampsia.

Transition—The end of the first stage of labor when dilatation of the cervix is between eight and ten centimeters and contractions are longest, strongest, and closest together. As soon as the baby's head has passed through the cervix, transition and the first stage of labor are over and the second stage has begun. Transition comprises about one-eighth of the total time in labor.

Trimester—A three-month period of time in pregnancy. The pregnancy is divided into three phases: first trimester, second trimester and third trimester.

Umbilical cord—The lifeline of the fetus. It is attached to the abdomen of the fetus and to the placenta. It is through the cord that the fetus passes wastes to the mother and receives nutrients and oxygen from her.

Umbilicus—The scar or mark left on the baby where the umbilical cord has fallen off after it is cut. Also known as the navel or "belly button."

Urethra—The canal that carries urine from the bladder to the outside of the body.

Uterus—The muscular organ in which the fetus develops. Also known as the womb.

Vacuum extraction—A technique developed in Sweden to aid in the removal of the fetus from the birth canal; used in place of forceps.

Vagina—The birth canal.

Vernix—The cheese-like protective material that covers the baby's skin while in the uterus.

Vertex—The top of the head.

Bibliography

Books About Fathering

Boston Women's Health Collective. *Ourselves and Our Children.* New York: Random House, 1978.

Dodson, Fitzhugh. *How to Father.* New York: New American Library, 1974.

______. *How to Parent.* New York: Signet Books, 1970.

Elkins, Valmai. *The Rights of the Pregnant Parent.* Ottawa: Waxwing Productions, 1976.

English, Spurgeon, and Foster, Constance. *A Guide to Successful Fatherhood.* Chicago: Science Research Associates, 1954.

Farrell, Warren. *The Liberated Man.* New York: Random House, 1975.

Green, Maureen. *Fathering.* New York: McGraw-Hill, 1976.

Leboyer, Frederick. *Loving Hands.* New York: Alfred A. Knopf, 1976.

Mayle, Peter. *How to Be a Pregnant Father.* New Jersey: Lyle Stuart Inc., 1977.

Phillips, C. and Anzalone, J.. *Fathering.* St. Louis: C.V. Mosby Company, 1978.

Salk, Lee. *Preparing for Parenthood.* New York: David McKay Co., Inc., 1974.

Salk, Lee, and Kramer, Rita. *How to Raise a Human Being.* New York: Random House, 1969.

Schaefer, George. *The Expectant Father.* New York: Barnes and Noble Books, 1972.

Films About Fathering

The Nurturing Father, a film produced by Media for Childbirth Education, P.O. Box 2092, Castro Valley, California 94546.

Pregnant Fathers, a film produced by the Joseph T. Anzalone Foundation, P.O. Box 5206, Santa Cruz, California 95063.

Fathers, a film produced by Durrin Films for ASPO, 1411 K St., N.W., Washington, D.C. 20005.

Books About Pregnancy

Bing, Elisabeth. *Moving Through Pregnancy.* New York: Bobbs-Merrill, 1975.

Bing, Elisabeth and Colman, Libby. *Making Love During Pregnancy.* New York: Bantam Books, 1977.

Curtis, Lindsay, and Caroler, Yvonne. *Pregnant and Loving It.* Tucson, Arizona: HP Books, 1977.

Davis, M. Edward, and Maisel, Edward. *Have Your Baby, Keep Your Figure.* New York: Essandess Special Editions, 1963.

Dilfer, Carol. *Your Baby, Your Body.* New York: Crown Publishers, Inc., 1977.

Gillespie, Clark. *Your Pregnancy Month by Month.* New York: Harper and Row, Publishers, 1977.

Gots, Ronald and Barbara. *Caring for Your Unborn Child.* New York: Stein and Day Publishers, 1977.

Hartman, Rhondda. *Exercises for True Natural Childbirth.* New York: Harper and Row, Publishers, 1975.

Leboyer, Frederick. *Inner Beauty, Inner Light.* New York: Alfred A. Knopf, 1978.

Marzollo, Jean. *Nine Months, One Day, One Year.* New York: Harper and Row, Publishers, 1973.

McCauley, Carole. *Pregnancy after 35.* New York: D.P. Dutton and Co., Inc., 1976.

Morton, Marcia. *Pregnancy Notebook.* New York: Workman Publishing Co., 1972.

Noble, Elizabeth. *Essential Exercises for the Childbearing Year.* Boston: Houghton Mifflin Company, 1976.

Nurnberg, Maxwell, and Rosenblum, Morris. *What To Name Your Baby.* New York: Collier Books, 1962.

Trimmer, Eric. *Having a Baby.* New York: St. Martin's Press, 1974.

Weller, Stella. *Easy Pregnancy With Yoga.* Vancouver, Canada: Fforbez Enterprises Ltd., 1978.

Books About Childbirth

Bean, Constance. *Labor and Delivery: An Observer's Diary.* New York: Doubleday & Company, Inc., 1977.

______. *Methods of Childbirth.* New York: Dolphin Books, 1974.

Bing, Elisabeth. *Six Practical lessons For An Easier Childbirth.* New York: Grosset & Dunlap, 1967.

Brennan, Barbara. *The Complete Book of Midwifery.* New York: Dutton & Co., Inc., 1977.

Brook, Dana. *Naturebirth.* New York: Pantheon Books, 1976.

Dick-Read, Grantly. *Childbirth Without Fear.* New York: Harper and Row, Publishers, 1959.

______. *The Natural Childbirth Primer.* New York: Harper & Row, Publishers, 1955.

Donovan, Bonnie. *The Cesarean Birth Experience.* Boston: Beacon Press, 1977.

Ewy, Donna, and Ewy Roger. *Preparation for Childbirth.* New York: Signet Books, 1970.

Gold, Cybele, and Gold, E.J. *Joyous Childbirth.* Berkeley, California: And/Or Press, 1977.

Karmel, Marjorie. *Thank You, Dr. Lamaze.* New York: Dolphin Books, 1959.

Kitzinger, Sheila. *Giving Birth.* New York: Taplinger Publishing Company, 1971.

Lamaze, Fernand. *Painless Childbirth: The Lamaze Method.* New York: Pocket Books, 1974.

Lang, Raven. *Birth Book.* Palo Alto, California: Genesis Press, 1972.

Leboyer, Frederick. *Birth Without Violence.* New York: Alfred A. Knopf, 1975.

LeShan, Eda. *Natural Parenthood.* New York: Signet Books, 1970.

Macfarlane, Aidan. *The Psychology of Childbirth.* Cambridge, Massachusetts: Harvard University Press, 1977.

MacMahon, Alice. *All About Childbirth.* Maitland, Florida: Family Publications, 1978.

Tanzer, Deborah. *Why Natural Childbirth.* New York: Schocken Books, 1976.

Tucker, Tarvez. *Prepared Childbirth.* New Canaan, Connecticut: Tobey Publishing Co., Inc., 1975.

Vellay, Pierre. *Childbirth With Confidence.* New York: The MacMillan Company, 1965.

______. *Childbirth Without Pain.* New York: E.P. Dutton & Co., Inc., 1960.

Wright, Erna. *The New Childbirth.* New York: Pocket Books, 1971.

Books About Breastfeeding

Gerard, Alice. *Please Breastfeed Your Baby.* New York: Signet Books, 1970.

LaLeche League. *The Womanly Art of Breastfeeding.* Franklin Park, Illinois: La Leche League International, 1963.

Pryor, Karen. *Nursing Your Baby.* New York: Pocket Books, 1963.

Raphael, Dana. *The Tender Gift: Breastfeeding.* New York: Schocken Books, 1978.

Index

M

N

P

Q

R

S

T

U

V